T0300323

Routledge Revivals

The Third Oil Shock

First published in 1983, this book collects a number of essays about the effects of a sustained period of low oil prices. The opening chapter describes how oil prices have impinged on other elements of the economy and assesses the costs and benefits, in the short and long term, of low prices. The following three chapters deal with different groups of countries and indicate clearly that for none of them do lower oil prices have unequivocally positive or negative effects — a situation examined in the chapter on the international financial system. The last three chapters analyse the shifts lower prices are likely to produce in relations among the groups closely involved in the oil market.

The Third Oil Shock

The Effects of Lower Oil Prices

Edited by
Joan Pearce

Routledge
Taylor & Francis Group

First published in 1983
by Routledge & Kegan Paul

This edition first published in 2016 by Routledge
2 Park Square, Milton Park, Abingdon, Oxon, OX14 4RN
and by Routledge
711 Third Avenue, New York, NY 10017

Routledge is an imprint of the Taylor & Francis Group, an informa business

© 1983 Royal Institute of International Affairs

All rights reserved. No part of this book may be reprinted or reproduced or
utilised in any form or by any electronic, mechanical, or other means, now
known or hereafter invented, including photocopying and recording, or in any
information storage or retrieval system, without permission in writing from the
publishers.

Publisher's Note
The publisher has gone to great lengths to ensure the quality of this reprint but
points out that some imperfections in the original copies may be apparent.

Disclaimer
The publisher has made every effort to trace copyright holders and welcomes
correspondence from those they have been unable to contact.

A Library of Congress record exists under LC control number: 83211138

ISBN 13: 978-1-138-66596-5 (hbk)
ISBN 13: 978-1-315-61807-4 (ebk)

CHATHAM HOUSE SPECIAL PAPER

The Third Oil Shock

The Effects of Lower Oil Prices

Edited by
Joan Pearce

The Royal Institute of International Affairs

Routledge & Kegan Paul
London, Boston and Henley

This paper forms part of the Institute's international economic programme.

The Royal Institute of International Affairs is an unofficial body which promotes the scientific study of international questions and does not express opinions of its own. The opinions expressed in this paper are the responsibility of the authors.

First published 1983
by Routledge & Kegan Paul Ltd
39 Store Street, London WC1E 7DD,
9 Park Street, Boston, Mass. 02108, USA, and
Broadway House, Newtown Road,
Henley-on-Thames, Oxon RG9 1EN

Reproduced from copy supplied
Printed in Great Britain by
Billing & Son Ltd, Worcester

© Royal Institute of International Affairs 1983

No part of this book may be reproduced in
any form without permission from the
publisher except for the quotation of brief
passages in criticism

ISBN 0-7102-0079-X

Contents

Preface

Towards the end of 1982 the price of oil was the subject of much attention. The discussion concentrated on whether the price of oil would fall, by how much and for how long. Little consideration was given to what would be the effects on the world political economy if the price of oil were to decline significantly and not to rise again for a sustained period. The probability of this materializing seemed high enough, and the consequences if it did important enough, to make it worth examining in some detail. Hence, earlier this year I asked a number of experts to write not about what would happen to oil prices but about what would happen if lower oil prices were to prevail for some time. The result is this book. Although by the time these chapters were written the London Agreement of March 1983 had brought closer the prospect of enduring lower prices, the authors treat that prospect as a hypothesis rather than as an established fact.

Oil is a large enough element in the international economy for a major change in the trend of oil prices to have widespread repercussions. Lower oil prices alone will not change the course of the world economy, nor indeed of most national economies. They will rather curb or hasten existing impetus; at the margin this can be highly signficant. In the context of economic activity in the industrial countries, lower oil prices will not in themselves cause a recovery, but if there is already an incipient recovery lower oil prices will make it more vigorous and longer-lasting.

The opening chapter describes how oil prices have impinged on other elements of the economy and assesses the costs and benefits, in the short and longer runs, that could flow from lower oil prices. The following three chapters deal with different groups of countries and indicate clearly that for none of them do lower oil prices represent either an unalloyed boon or an outright calamity. A case in which lower oil prices could tip the balance is considered in the chapter on the international financial system. The last three chapters analyse the shifts that lower prices are likely to produce in relations among those groups most closely involved in the oil market: the extent of OPEC's influence; the consumer countries' need for energy security; and the altered role of the oil industry.

I am very grateful to the authors for having written to a tight, in some cases a very tight, deadline, and for responding with alacrity to my queries and suggestions. From the outset I have received guidance from Robert Belgrave, head of the British Institutes' Joint Energy Programme. He and most of the authors, together with Roy Batchelor, Alastair Clark, Richard Portes and Patricia Romines met early in May to discuss the chapters in draft. All of them, as well as Esperanza Duran, gave valuable advice. The production of this book owes much to the skilful diligence of Pauline Wickham. We appreciate the cooperation and flexibility of the staff of the Policy Studies Institute who set up the text on their word processor. As with many Chatham House enterprises, this one could not have been accomplished as quickly and as smoothly were it not for the outstanding competence and commitment of the secretaries; particular thanks are due to Louise Orrock and Jean Pell.

JP
May 1983

1 An Overview: Gains, Costs and Dilemmas
Edward L. Morse

OPEC agreed collectively to reduce official selling prices for the first time in its history in March 1983. The organization also imposed an overall production ceiling on its members and adopted a prorationing agreement, making the Saudis the explicit swing producer and market balancer. The price cut came in the midst of a political and intellectual debate concerning the fundamental evolution of the international energy sector. A host of questions has now arisen striking at some of the most basic and previously unchallenged assumptions about the 'rules' of the international 'oil game', the structure of the energy market-place and the evolving petroleum investment climate.

The essays in this volume take as a working assumption that there will be lower, but stable, oil prices for an extended period of a decade or more. They attempt to trace some of the likely implications of this assumption. The basis of the assumption is that the steep price increases of the 1970s have set in motion dynamic processes and structural changes in the global energy economy which will effectively preclude prices higher than at present for a decade or so. Demand has fallen partly as a result of the global recession, but probably more significantly because of long-term structural changes associated with conservation in most user sectors, inter-fuel substitution, new investment and inventory patterns, and the proliferation of participants in the oil markets.

Whether this working assumption is borne out depends on a variety of factors, about which we know little today. There are no good data on which to base projections of demand or supply. Lower prices should cause demand to increase and the development of new supplies to lag, but the magnitude of both responses is unclear. Similarly, whether there is price stability or greater volatility depends on whether OPEC remains cohesive and able to influence the market.

Despite these unknowns, it seems useful to assume that

1

price stability at the new levels will persist, in order to trace the benefits and costs. Even this is by no means easy. Modestly declining prices are generally agreed to offer, overall, a positive and well-timed fillip to the world economy, but other implications of lower prices are unclear. The downward price adjustments of 1983 have positive and notable impacts both on efforts to bring world inflation under control and on recovery from the staggering international recession which earlier price increases, themselves, helped to bring about. In the United States alone, a four-dollar reduction in price adds the equivalent of more than $20 billion to disposable income - about the same order of impact as the first two years of the Reagan Administration's reductions in personal income tax! It reduces directly the USA's import bill by more than $10 billion and the import bills of the rest of the world by at least $25 billion(1).

In the short run, these general and diffuse positive benefits to most governments and consumers should be set against the more concentrated costs to all oil-exporting countries. Over the longer term, however, the situation could be reversed if under-investment in new conventional energy supplies combines with dramatic increases in demand to put in place the structural conditions for another round of price rises.

This balance of costs and benefits between exporters and importers is reflected in the international financial system, with some debtor countries' problems intensifying as those of others are alleviated. Similarly, in the trading system: the oil price reduction, by helping to foster growth in some countries, opens new trade opportunities; but, by reducing the income of oil exporters, it constricts their markets for imports from industrial and developing countries alike, depriving exporters of markets (for capital goods, armaments, consumer goods and agricultural products) which were previously growing robustly at the very time when international trade was generally stagnating. The overall balance is hard to assess.

Also imponderable is the degree to which the recent price reductions both reflect and feed a process of rapid and fundamental structural change in the international petroleum economy. Much depends on how great a role OPEC continues to play. This will be determined by whether the organization holds together despite a situation which exacerbates its internal tensions; whether it can collaborate with non-OPEC oil-exporting countries; and whether its share of world oil production capacity continues to decline. Another important factor is the tendency of the petroleum sector to behave more like 'normal' commodity markets. It is unclear how far this tendency will continue, and whether consumer or producer governments will want or will be able to prevent the market elements from dominating the administered elements in the oil sector. A last major uncertainty is whether future investment conditions will encourage enough energy investment to obviate a further period of supply shortage.

The cyclical nature of the oil market

Governments, energy-intensive sectors of the economy and, perhaps most of all, the oil industry were caught off guard when the oil supply overhang emerged. Most analysts had confidently argued that the world was in the midst of a two-to-three-decade period in which there would be a precarious balance between supply and demand for petroleum while alternative fuels were being developed(2). On the premise that oil demand would for some time outstrip new discoveries of conventional petroleum, prices were expected to increase annually by inflation plus about 2%. This view was reinforced by the particular vulnerability of oil supply to disruption due to civil strife or regional conflict in or among oil-producing countries, or by reason of Soviet intervention.

How could such a sizeable glut have emerged between 1979 and 1982? Apparent demand for oil in the non-communist world was over 51 million barrels per day (b/d) in 1979, and fell to less than 41 million b/d by the end of 1982, with demand for OPEC oil falling from 31 million b/d to less than 15 million b/d, reducing OPEC's market share from over 63% to about 33%. Is cyclicality something new in the oil markets?

Cyclicality in the oil markets - fluctuations in demand or supply with accompanying changes in prices - has always existed. But, because the short-run elasticity of both demand for and supply of oil are low (that is, demand and supply respond slowly to price changes) and because oil prices have often been controlled in some way, by companies or by governments, this cyclicality has not been evident. The sustained real price increases of the past decade obscured those qualities which make oil similar to other commodities, while emphasizing qualities which seemed to make petroleum unique.

Evidence of cyclical fluctuations can be found in what might be called the first international oil regime, which lasted roughly from 1928 to 1971, and in the second regime in the 1970s(3). In the first period, both the nominal and the

3

real price of oil steadily declined as inexpensive new fields were brought onstream, principally in the Middle East. The oil regime was dominated by the Seven Sisters, the large integrated oil majors, which were responsible for exploration, production, refining and marketing worldwide. These few vertically integrated actors in the market-place managed cyclical changes in demand by adjusting production in the exporting countries, whose resources they controlled. Cyclical changes, in short, were almost wholly absorbed by producing/exporting countries. Indeed, countering this undue burden of adjustment, along with a redistribution of the 'rents' from oil, were the primary incentives behind OPEC's formation.

The regime of the 1970s had a more complex set of mechanisms to deal with changes in demand, as OPEC successfully administered prices and increased its share of the rents from oil operations. OPEC broke the control of the vertically integrated companies over resources in the ground, and quickly changed the nature of the market, by shifting the burden of cyclical adjustment to the companies and the consuming country societies. It also attempted to move vigorously into downstream operations, competing directly with the majors in selling and distributing crude and drawing up ambitious plans in refining and petrochemicals. But OPEC's actions also laid the basis for its demise. New players entered the game, vastly increasing the number of actors in the market-place and developing non-OPEC sources of exports. And, an array of national oil companies, in both the developing and the industrial countries, assisted by government subsidies, further eroded the roles both of the majors and of OPEC governments in finding new crude sources, in purchasing crude outside established channels, and in creating new distribution and other downstream operations.

Inexorably, it seemed, the transformation in the petroleum economy during the 1960s and 1970s would lead to a public-sector-dominated arrangement with many players replacing a predominantly private sector market, dominated by a few participants. The bargaining relationship between private firms and governments shifted dramatically in favour of the latter, as the concession system was effectively terminated and replaced by production-sharing arrangements. Indeed, it appeared to many observers that the ineluctable trend was reducing the role of private firms to service or risk-contract arrangements, with exploitation and distribution becoming the exclusive domain of governments.

But such assumptions about the underlying structure of the international oil market have now been undermined. Only four years after the world had succumbed to two oil shocks within seven years, a period of over-capacity in production developed, unexpectedly, but for reasons inherent in the OPEC arrangements.

Cyclical changes are now being manifested in ways more typical of a normal commodity market, with prices more reflective of the basic balance between supply and demand. OPEC's unwillingness to relinquish the goals and roles that it established in the 1970s has placed its members back in the position they were in before 1973. Once again it is they who have borne an undue share of the cyclical adjustment.

The decline of OPEC and the reassertion of the supply-and-demand balance as the major determinant of oil prices signify the reappearance of a 'normal' market in the international petroleum economy. Its scope and durability will depend to some degree on how long the current oil glut will last and whether OPEC will, politically, be able to administer a floor price, a question to which we will return later. But other changes in the structure of the world petroleum economy have halted and will almost inevitably reverse the trends of the 1960s and 1970s. Private petroleum companies are now re-emerging as the main players in the petroleum game, albeit in ways significantly different from those of the 1950s.

The economic factors responsible for the recent price reductions - the phenomenal 20% decline in free world consumption over three years and the dramatically increased supply overhang - are well documented(4). These factors include: the worldwide economic recession; conservation stemming from a decade of steep price increases; the drawdown by companies of their historically high inventory levels, at what were probably unprecedented rates; the increase in non-OPEC supplies to 22 million b/d, and the preference of companies to buy from these more competitive and secure sources; and inter-fuel competition, with the substitution of oil by coal, natural gas and nuclear energy. While the weighting of these factors is open to dispute, my view is that the recession is the least important; conservation, new oil supplies outside of OPEC, and structural change in the industrial economies account for most of the change. Hence economic factors will prevent the price of oil from rising in real terms for the rest of the decade. Political factors will be required to prevent the price from falling.

Assessing the impact of the recession is difficult, as is

differentiating between the effects of recession and conservation. There used to be a close relationship between energy consumption and economic growth, with the two increasing on a 1:1 basis for most of this century. But 1973 marked a break in this historical linkage. The International Energy Agency(5), for example, estimates that for the eight years after 1973, when OECD growth averaged 2.3% per annum, the demand for energy barely increased (by 0.2% annually). Substantial savings were found in every sector of the economies of the industrial countries, led by housing and transportation, followed by the commercial and industrial sectors. At the same time quite rapid structural adjustment occurred, which entailed capital expenditure shifting from such energy-intensive sectors as steel and cement and towards light industry, services and energy conservation. How an upturn in economic activity would affect the relationship is uncertain. As for conservation, this should not be much less with oil priced at $29 than at $34 or $40, so long as the perception remains that oil prices will increase in the long run. (On the other hand, investments in unconventional alternative fuels will continue to be uneconomic.) There is, in fact, growing evidence that the conservation gains manifested in the late 1970s and early 1980s stemmed from the price increases of 1973-4 and that the gains from the 1979-80 price increases have not yet worked through the major economies.

Inventory patterns present similar unknowns. The first half of 1982 saw an unprecedented inventory drawdown worldwide due to lower prices, high interest rates and lower demand. Contrary to expectations, inventory reductions accelerated into the first quarter of 1983, when they reached perhaps over 5.5 million b/d (vs. historical seasonal levels of 1.5-2.5 million b/d). This drawdown increased excess supply and helped accelerate the downward price movement. The drawdown will eventually end, but it is hard to say that inventories will now be carried at any specific level, other than the number of days of forward consumption required by some governments. Ready access to additional supplies and uncertainty over the evolution of prices will probably mean that once inventories are stabilized, they will not undergo their historical seasonal variance.

Inventory management has in the recent past reinforced the trend of demand. During the tightening market conditions of 1979-81, inventories were built to historically high levels, helping to sustain the upward price movement. The opposite has been the case since 1981. If in future the oil market is going to behave increasingly like that of an

6

ordinary commodity, with more frequent price variations, inventory management may serve to dampen, rather than to amplify, price variability. Importing country governments, consumers, producer-companies and producer-governments all have a stake in this. OPEC ministers would like inventory or stock policy to head the agenda of a global dialogue.

Fuel substitution has clearly reduced demand. The share of oil in overall energy consumption, after increasing dramatically from 40% in 1960 to 56% in 1973, has steadily declined, giving way, especially in the OECD countries, to coal (for which demand rose twice as fast after 1973 than before), nuclear energy and, to a lesser degree, natural gas.

On the supply side, the momentum of the 1970s seems likely to continue into the 1980s, with non-OPEC exploration and development outpacing progress in OPEC countries. Since 1973 OPEC reserves have grown by less than 0.5% annually (as against 6% before), compared with 4% for non-OPEC reserves (2.6% before). Many believe this trend will continue. Conoco, for example, forecasts non-OPEC supplies increasing to 28 million b/d by 1990, despite the expected decline in Soviet exports. With oil demand worldwide increasing at no more than 1% a year for the next twenty years, demand on OPEC is not expected to exceed 22 million b/d throughout the 1980s and 26-27 million b/d in the 1990s.

Whether oil will lose all of its unique aspects remains open. Few sectors of the economy have been more politicized than energy. In neither the industrial nor the developing countries, in neither OPEC nor non-OPEC members is there yet a clear consensus on the degree to which energy, and petroleum in particular, should be integrated into the public sector. Providing energy security - access to reliable, uninterruptible sources of energy at reasonable prices to consumers - is widely accepted as a public responsibility in the consuming countries. But the mixture of private and public initiative with respect to exploration, development and production, distribution and pricing of fuels has been a hotly debated political subject and is likely to remain so. Much depends on whether - and, if so, when and under what conditions - a new supply disruption takes place. Much depends as well on how the longer-term investment cycle, which accompanies the shorter-term demand and supply cycle, is played out.

The petroleum investment cycle
Investment patterns in the petroleum industry reflect the interplay of a multiplicity of factors: geology, projected

prices and costs, availability of capital, terms and conditions for entry established by 'host' governments, and expected stability of economic and political conditions and of governmental policies. As with all structural changes in a key sector, the bases of one investment regime are established in its predecessor. What has undermined the regime of the 1970s was the discovery of large reservoirs of oil outside of OPEC; many of these discoveries were in the industrial country market-places of Europe and North America, where governments have historically been uncomfortable with administered pricing and unwilling to establish production limitations in order to support price levels. These non-OPEC discoveries were the necessary conditions for what is transpiring in the 1980s. The sufficient conditions were the supply overhang and political decisions taken in the United States.

Clearly, the most important of these is the decision taken in the United States to decontrol the prices of crude oil and petroleum products. OPEC's rise to power related not only to overall oil market conditions, but also to the change in the United States' position in the world petroleum economy as it moved from net self-sufficiency to the distinctive position of the world's largest importer of crude oil. That transformation was accelerated and accentuated by the imposition of price controls in 1974.

Price controls were designed to buffer the US economy from oil-pricing decisions taken 'outside' the United States. The system worked perversely, encouraging oil imports, increasing the vulnerability of the United States and of other importing countries to a supply disruption at a time when reducing both should have been the primary goals of energy policy. It increased frictions with other importing countries, virtually all of which priced oil at market levels, or, through their fiscal systems, higher. It discouraged domestic exploration and resulted in misallocation of domestic resources because it sent the wrong price signals to consumers and investors.

The decision to decontrol oil prices reversed all of the perverse consequences of maintaining lower than world prices in the US market-place. It was followed by a dramatic reduction in oil imports, from over 8 million b/d to under 3 million b/d for a brief period, and had a permanent impact on the trajectory of US oil demand. The decontrol of US prices, more importantly, enabled the United States to become reintegrated into the world petroleum economy, shifting pricing power away from OPEC and towards the largest consumer market-place and unleashing an oil investment

8

boom in the United States that affected investment patterns worldwide.

The United States has always attracted a disproportionate share of petroleum investment, even during the period of price controls in the 1970s. After 1979, this share grew even larger - 85% or more of active rigs were onshore or offshore the United States in 1980-2. With price decontrol, the United States became the most attractive investment climate for three simple reasons.

First, the United States offers an unparalleled combination of political stability and economic liberalism. Second, its fiscal regime is far more attractive than most others. Third, despite the extraordinary amount of drilling which has occurred historically in the United States, the potential for large discoveries offshore the United States remains great.

The reduced profit horizon of companies associated with the recession and the decline in world oil prices, combined with the new attractive investment climate in the United States, is creating a competition for petroleum investment capital which could well transform the rules of the investment game internationally. What we can expect to see for the remainder of this decade is a reversal of what took place in the past decade, with an improvement - perhaps a dramatic improvement - in the investment terms provided by governments to private oil companies as those foreign governments realize how much they need to compete with the United States to attract petroleum investments.

The 1960s and 1970s were clearly a period of petroleum nationalism. Oil and mining companies were expropriated, and the concession system was replaced by production-sharing agreements and a movement to service or fixed-fee contracts. In most cases, a government was assumed to own its country's oil and mineral resources, which became regarded as precious depletable elements of national sovereignty. Competition among companies for access to crude oil allowed governments to impose increasingly stringent terms on those wishing to explore for and produce oil, as well as to feel able, in many cases, to change contractual terms unilaterally in order to increase their take.

The situation has been rapidly reversed. For the rest of this decade governments will be competing with each other for oil company capital and, in particular, competing against the standard set by the investment climate in the United States. This trend, which I believe will accelerate, began, perhaps, in 1980 when the military government of Peru relinquished power to a democratically elected regime eager to reinvigorate the national petroleum sector. To attract companies, in the aftermath of widespread nationalization by the military, terms competitive with those in the United States were offered. By now, Peru has been joined by perhaps a dozen countries in relaxing the terms for investment. The North Sea countries are actively reviewing their fiscal systems, and the United Kingdom has already taken steps to alter its investment climate so as to foster continued petroleum exploration and development.

The most important question in assessing foreign investment risks and opportunities is whether this improvement will be permanent, or whether it will be changed unilaterally and retroactively by individual governments when the next oil shortage occurs. The answer will depend on other international developments, and on how wisely oil companies and governments devise stable contractual terms for exploration and development, which will withstand the cyclical forces of rising and falling oil demand.

There are other lessons about the sanctity of contractual obligations and commitments, which could carry over into the next pricing cycle. Those countries which unilaterally voided contracts when oil prices were escalating were the first to suffer when companies and even government purchasing agents voided or cancelled agreements as oil prices started to fall. Interest in the sanctity of contracts may well revive, prompting measures to make government promises more credible.

A more important change, perhaps, is the growth in multinational activities by the national oil companies of oil-producing countries, and especially their interest in investing in exploration and production in the United States and even in some OPEC countries. The Kuwait Petroleum Company is a case in point, with its upstream and downstream investments in the United States, Indonesia, China and Western Europe. One of the most significant effects of a period of stable and low prices could be to accelerate this trend. It would revive interest in formalizing reciprocity of investment terms and would deter governments from changing contracts unilaterally.

OPEC's choices
Some of the major consequences of lower prices are felt by OPEC, and OPEC's own responses to lower prices are critical to the future paths that prices might follow. Stable prices can be anticipated only if OPEC is able to maintain its cohesion, and, as Louis Turner argues later in this volume,

10

this is much doubted. If any of OPEC's major members decides to strike out on its own, aiming to increase its market share by offering lower prices, the organization might disintegrate, with prices falling steeply and a new era of price volatility ensuing.

Three main issues are debated in relation to OPEC. Primary is the question whether OPEC did in the past, or can in the future, determine prices. Second is OPEC's cohesion and the degree to which members' interests are mutual or divisive. Third is Saudi Arabia's role in the organization and whether it is dominant or dominated by the others.

OPEC's 'power' has probably been overstated in the past, just as it has been understated more recently. With production capacity of something over 31 million b/d, OPEC is apparently best able to administer prices and maintain internal cohesion when demand for OPEC production is in the 24-26 million b/d range. When demand is higher, there have historically been overwhelming incentives for individual members to break out from the OPEC pack by extracting higher prices via premia and spot market sales. When demand is lower, discounts and spot sales are offered to increase market shares. Opportunities for exacting premia or offering discounts have been far more frequent than periods of OPEC cohesion. In this sense, OPEC has been less a price administrator than a follower of market tendencies.

This view, however, depreciates the overall impact that OPEC has had on prices. Official prices are many times greater than production costs throughout the Middle East: only OPEC's willingness to impose a prorationing programme has prevented prices from falling dramatically. Similarly in past periods of tightness, only OPEC's general agreement on a marker price has restrained prices from rising well above the levels actually set. OPEC has not been a paper organization. Whether it can maintain its pricing and production role depends most on whether demand for OPEC oil picks up and attains the 24-26 million b/d level before too many of its members offer competitive discounts and the pressures on the organization's coherence become overwhelming. OPEC's major test in an era of lower prices is whether, having ceased to be a price administrator, it can act as a price preserver.

OPEC's cohesion is a function of a number of related factors: its overall market share, the commonality of interests of its members, and politics among the members of the organization. OPEC's cohesion depends largely on its reasserting its market presence following the phenomenal and unprecedented drop in its share of oil consumption in the non-

11

communist world - from 63% to 33% - during the past few years.

In the short term, a rebound in demand can result only from an end to inventory drawdown and a spurt in economic activity in the industrial world. At best, however, demand for OPEC oil will probably not be as much as 21 million b/d until 1984-5. In this case, OPEC's members will undergo significant and perhaps unprecedented pressures to discount, as Louis Turner argues below. This does not mean that OPEC will necessarily fall apart. Its members may well be up to the task, depending largely on what sacrifices Saudi Arabia and some other producers are willing to endure for the sake of OPEC unity.

The longer-term outlook is equally problematic. It is generally recognized that while OPEC will be able to recoup some of its lost market share, it will be hard pressed to regain its former level. Moreover, declining production, combined with increased domestic demand in many OPEC members, will radically shift their relative positions. As Edwin A. Deagle, Jr, has recently pointed out(6), Algeria, Ecuador, Gabon and Qatar may well drop out of OPEC's ranks by 1990, with limited, if any, export capacity. Four others - Indonesia, Libya, Nigeria and Venezuela - will probably export substantially less than at their peak, with little or no capacity to modify their production as part of an OPEC production programme. OPEC's rump would, in these circumstances, compromise the five Persian Gulf countries, whose total production capacity would be no more than 24 million b/d. Power within OPEC would be concentrated in the Gulf countries.

Awareness of these eventualities has enabled OPEC's members to maintain their cohesion as a group despite formidable temptations for individual countries to break ranks. None of them has an interest in price volatility; none wishes market forces to predominate over intervention in the market-place. But their unity on these general objectives conceals profound differences in other respects. High reserve, low population countries (Saudi Arabia in particular, Kuwait and the UAE to a lesser degree), taking a long-term view, desire price stability and price moderation in order to stretch out the life of their reserves and to preserve both the role of oil in energy consumption and OPEC's share of world oil trade. The low reserve, high population countries, taking a short-term view, wish to maximize income so as to accelerate industrialization, in preparation for the imminent decline in their exports, and to service their debt. They generally prefer price hawkishness, but in present circumstances they are the most likely to offer discounts in order to increase volumes to be exported and thereby enhance revenues.

Over time, if OPEC power becomes focused on a small group of Gulf countries, the stresses on the group are likely to increase, and its internal and external policy postures are likely to change. The smaller OPEC/Gulf group will undoubtedly desire to maintain price stability, although Iran and Iraq, once their war is settled, will probably be more price hawkish. Market stabilization is likely to require enormous swings in production if the group is to assume the role of market balancer by itself(7).

The OPEC countries may find this impossible without coordinating policies both with the major non-OPEC producers and with the major importers. Recognizing the difficulties, some, especially the Gulf producers, endeavoured to begin a 'dialogue' with the major non-OPEC producers, the United Kingdom, Norway and Mexico, in March 1983, and hinted at willingness to have a dialogue with the USSR. Eventually, such a dialogue would need to involve also Japan, the United States and Germany.

Clearly, the best hope is to enlarge OPEC's ranks by enlisting Mexico. Mexico's choices here are quite difficult. Besides being averse to relinquishing national sovereignty over oil decisions to OPEC or any other group, the government also prefers to be a free rider on OPEC with respect to pricing, and to sell all it can produce. Mexico will have to be convinced that to restrict production is in its national interest before it becomes one of the market balancers. It is inconceivable that Norway or Britain would follow suit, except perhaps to exchange information on future increases in production capacity and to reach tacit agreements on pricing.

To obtain help in sharing the burdens of balancing supply and demand, OPEC will have to discuss market stabilization with the major consuming/importing countries with a view to achieving a commodity stabilization arrangement. As many of the OPEC/Gulf country oil ministers now realize, a dialogue will have to focus on stock management and prices in the domestic market-places of the consumers. But there is, and will continue to be, an aversion in the United States and the other industrial countries to the massive intervention which would be required. A fruitful dialogue on stock management is exceedingly unlikely in the current political environment.

Central to OPEC's cohesion is Saudi Arabia. There has been tension between it and the other members since the early 1970s when Saudi Arabian production and export capacity was expanded beyond any reasonable view of Saudi needs and in excess of that of any other OPEC country. The Saudis, with the largest export capacity and largest reserves in the world, have wanted to preserve as long as possible the importance of oil in the energy economy, of OPEC in the oil market, and of Saudia Arabia in OPEC. All these require price moderation, so the Saudis seek to maintain a gradually increasing real oil price. They have also wanted to depoliticize the process of price determination by relying as much as possible on presumptive rules of automaticity - they abhor confrontation(8).

OPEC currently faces two fundamental short-term challenges, both involving its core members. First, there is the question of how the burden of OPEC's market balancing role is to be spread within OPEC. Second, there is the political instability engendered by the combination of the oil glut and the continuing pressures of the Iranian revolution and the Iran/Iraq war.

OPEC as a whole has borne the brunt of the adjustment in the glut by virtue of its collective residual supplier role. GNP in OPEC in 1983 will fall for the third year in a row. The OPEC current account surplus, in excess of $100 billion in 1980, has vanished and will not for the time being re-emerge. Tables 1.1 and 1.2 demonstrate the abrupt decline in OPEC country export earnings and the extraordinary debt-servicing problems of such members as Venezuela and Nigeria. They also demonstrate the exceptional sacrifices, in terms of vastly reduced expenditures and development programmes, that Saudi Arabia must endure as its contribution to balancing the market. There is a serious risk that one, or more, of OPEC's members will decide that it can no longer sustain the share of the burden allotted to it by the March 1983 agreement. When demand picks up OPEC may be threatened by a dispute about how the benefits should be distributed.

Stability will also be subject to pressures indigenous to the Middle East. Post-revolutionary Iran relentlessly pursues its war with Iraq and will apparently be willing to terminate hostilities only after the Iraqi leadership is removed. It has served notice that it will not desist in its efforts to challenge Saudi Arabia's leadership in both OPEC and the Gulf Region, with its desire for a higher market share. Both it and Iraq will want to increase oil exports after the war ends. At

Table 1.1   OPEC crude oil export earnings

Country	1981			1982			1983*		
	Ex-ports (mmbd)	Price ($/bl)	Oil earn-ings ($bn)	Ex-ports (mmbd)	Price ($/bl)	Oil earn-ings ($bn)	Ex-ports (mmbd)	Price ($/bl)	Oil earn-ings ($bn)
Nigeria	1.3	38.25	17.2	1.1	34.50	13.8	1.2	29.50	12.9
Indonesia	1.1	35.00	13.4	0.8	34.75	10.2	0.8	29.50	8.6
Venezuela	1.3	31.00	14.3	1.1	30.00	12.1	1.3	30.00	14.2
Iran	0.8	35.30	10.5	1.7	30.00	18.6	2.0	27.50	20.0
Algeria	0.5	36.50	6.9	0.5	35.50	6.5	0.6	30.50	6.7
Saudi Arabia	9.0	32.50	106.9	5.9	34.00	73.2	4.1	28.00	42.0
Kuwait	0.8	34.25	10.2	0.6	32.30	7.0	1.0	27.50	10.0
Libya	0.9	39.25	13.7	1.1	35.25	14.2	1.1	30.00	12.0
Iraq	0.7	35.70	9.1	0.7	34.90	8.9	1.1	29.00	11.6
Qatar	0.3	36.50	5.2	0.4	34.90	5.1	0.3	29.50	3.2
UAE	1.5	36.00	18.9	1.1	35.00	14.1	1.0	29.50	10.7
Ecuador	0.1	34.50	1.3	0.1	33.00	1.2	0.2	29.00	2.1
Gabon	0.1	34.50	1.6	0.1	34.25	1.4	0.2	29.00	2.1
TOTAL	18.4	34.09	229	15.0	33.57	182.0	14.9	-	156.1

* Estimate based on 17.7 million b/d for the year.

OPEC current account balance (billion):

1980	+	$108.1	
1981	+	$ 53.3	
1982	-	$ 10.0	
1983 (est.)	+	$ 6.2	(assuming average annual exports at the indicated levels - not likely given Q1 production levels in 1983)

15

Table 1.2   Main oil exporters: estimated financial position

	Production required for budgeted gvt spending in 1982	International reserves ($ billion)*		External debt December 1981 ($ billion)	
	Million b/d	Dec. 1981	Jan. 1983	Long-term public debt	Short-term commercia debt (due in 1982)
OPEC					
Algeria	0.9	3.7	2.2	17.5	1.5
Ecuador	0.2	0.6	0.3	5.0	2.3
Gabon	0.2	0.2	0.3	-	0.1
Indonesia	1.6	5.0	3.0	18.2	3.0
Iran	2.4	-	-	7.5	1.5
Iraq	2.0	-	-	22.0	4.3
Kuwait	0.9	4.1	5.6	-	4.7
Libya	1.2	9.0	7.0	-	1.0
Nigeria	1.6	3.9	1.3	8.0	2.0
Qatar	0.2	0.3	0.3	-	0.3
Saudi Arabia	7.3	32.2	27.9	-	4.6
UAE	1.1	3.2	3.1	-	3.3
Venezuela	2.2	8.2	6.0	19.0	16.1
Others					
Mexico	3.0	4.1	0.5	30.0	27.7
Norway	0.5	6.2	6.6	13.7	-

*   Excludes foreign assets.

Source: IMF, International Financial Statistics, xxxvi:4 (April 1983).

whose expense will these exports be made, if demand remains relatively flat? The ever-present danger, of course, is a further radicalization of politics in the Middle East as a result of the festering Israeli dispute and the combination of the Iranian revolution and the Iran/Iraq war. The demonstration effects of the successful Islamic 'revolution' in Iran have undermined the political legitimacy of regimes throughout the area, including Egypt, Iraq and Saudi Arabia. Will the reverberations of lower oil prices, in the form of lower development expenditures in Saudi Arabia and the Gulf states, if combined with a radicalization of politics in the region, usher in a change in these regimes? Or will lower expenditures result in a reduction in foreign workers and a consolidation of regime legitimacy? Far-reaching change is likely, but its direction is indeterminate.

The short-term balance
The longer-term aspects of structural change in the international petroleum economy have been highlighted because they set the context within which oil price reductions took place. We shall now seek to assess the short-term costs and benefits of lower prices to the major participants in the energy sector.

The benefits of lower real prices. There is little doubt that for the world economy as a whole stable, but lower, prices afford short-term benefits. Lower prices may well provide the basis for a balanced recovery of the world economy in a context of price stability, which would make most societies better off. These benefits are not difficult to enumerate. And they are a mirror image of the costs of the price increases of the 1970s, which imposed economic dislocations on virtually all consuming countries, including impacts on prices, growth and employment.

The initial benefits of a decrease in oil prices can be thought of either in terms of a shift in market power from producers to consumers, or in terms of an excise tax rebate. All oil-importing economies will benefit from this rebate; the degree will depend in part on how the exchange rate between their currency and the dollar evolves (a stronger dollar results in lower benefits outside the United States and vice versa). If oil consumption is flat this year, or rises by no more than 1-2%, the net effect of the March OPEC agreement will be a shift of some $40 billion from oil-exporting to oil-importing countries, or about $110 million per day this year alone. Three-quarters of this benefit will be received by the OECD countries (about 0.4% of GNP) and one quarter by the LDC importers. Among developing countries, as David Pearce points out in Chapter 3, a $10 billion import savings should be compared to a net non-OPEC LDC trade deficit of some $76 billion.

Consumption and investment should, therefore, be enhanced by the price reduction, depending on how much of the reduction is passed on to consumers by governments and refiners. Regardless of government actions, lower import costs should reduce inflation in the industrial countries by as much as 1% this year (depending on price adjustments in other fuels), providing an overall boost to real incomes and spending. A reduction in costs and an increase in consumer spending should, all other things being equal, also help to revive capital expenditure.

Expectations are that lower oil prices should reduce not only inflation but also inflationary expectations, thereby also facilitating a reduction in nominal interest rates, especially outside the United States. In the United States the electoral cycle should help, at least through 1984, to reverse the increase in real interest rates. Overall the reduction in oil prices should reinforce the decline in interest rates and promote other factors leading to at least a moderate economic recovery.

Government policies, both fiscal and monetary, will be important in determining the effects of lower oil prices. Governments in most industrial countries will be tempted to increase energy consumer taxes, principally to raise revenue, but also to compensate for the fall in oil prices and so maintain the momentum of energy conservation and the development of other fuels. If governments are short-sighted, however, they will not offset increases in energy consumer taxes by decreases in other taxes, including those whose reduction would foster energy development.

For industrial and developing countries, reduced oil import costs will improve the balance of payments, to the extent that they are not outweighed by other factors, including increases in oil imports (which probably will not be very great) and increases in other imports (which probably will be sizeable, but will - particularly if they are capital goods - help spur on world output and trade). Improved balance-of-payments positions will enhance developing countries' ability to service their debts and possibly persuade international banks to lend to them on more favourable terms.

The net imports of the dozen largest borrowers among oil-importing LDCs in 1982 were more than $30 billion. Lower oil prices should reduce these countries' import costs by about 15%, or $5 billion, benefiting especially Brazil, Turkey, Thailand, the Philippines and Korea[9]. The external debt of this group rose by some 10% to over $300 billion last year. Lower interest rates may reduce their debt-servicing charges by as much as $6 billion net this year.

It should be noted that oil demand in developing countries is relatively inelastic. Unlike the industrial countries, they use oil chiefly for essential purposes. They were thus unable to reduce their demand for oil during the price escalations of the past, but will probably not greatly increase it now that prices are lower.

Costs of declining real prices. The other side of the short-term balance sheet is no less pronounced, although the costs of declining prices are concentrated in the oil-exporting countries and the oil industry. There is an immediate cost for all LDC oil-exporting countries as a result of lower prices, although the non-OPEC exporters, and Mexico in particular, are better off than OPEC given their ability to market all available production. Even lower interest rates and enhanced non-oil exports cannot offset the abrupt and unexpected decline in export earnings from oil - which on average constitute over 80% of the OPEC countries' earnings (over 95% for some), and more than 50% for Mexico. The lost revenues will eventually result in a significant reduction of imports of both consumer and capital goods (dampening world trade), a curtailment of development programmes, an increase in indebtedness (perhaps imposing a greater burden on the international financial system), and a threat to domestic political authority.

Of course the burden of this adjustment will not be evenly spread, given the willingness of Saudi Arabia and the other Gulf countries to absorb, at least temporarily, a disproportionate share. The countries outside the Gulf will encounter difficulties which, though less severe than they might have been, will be more severe than those of the exporters with small populations and huge foreign asset holdings. The total external debt of the nine OPEC and non-OPEC oil-exporting developing countries outside the Gulf increased by about 40% between 1980 and 1982, to a level of more than $200 billion, of which more than 35% is due in 1983 (see Table 3). Even with lower interest rates, total net interest payments may remain at roughly the same level owing to increased debt, reduced earnings on foreign holdings, and the raising of the 'risk' element in their loan charges. Nor can most of these countries expect income from other sources to mitigate the deterioration in their current accounts. Only Mexico,

19

Table 1.3   Oil export earnings: implications of a $28 per barrel oil price for
             nine major borrowers

| | | Change in net oil exports in 1983 | |
	$ billions(a)	% of imports(b)	% of 1982 GNP
Indonesia	-2.3	10.7	2.5
Venezuela	-2.2	12.7	3.1
Nigeria	-1.7	10.0	2.5
Mexico	-1.5	6.5	0.9
Algeria	-1.3	9.6	3.2
Ecuador	-0.3	13.1	2.4
Malaysia	-0.2	1.3	0.8
Peru	-0.2	5.0	1.2
Egypt	-0.1	1.0	0.3

(a)   After adjustment for price differentials and export volume changes.
(b)   Goods and services, excluding oil and interest, before adjustment to lower
      oil earnings.

Source: World Financial Markets (New York, Morgan Guaranty Trust Co., April
          1983), p.10.

Indonesia and Malaysia will be able to benefit from growth in non-oil export earnings as the world economy rebounds.

The significant negative repercussions on the oil exporters of the decline in oil prices will be transmitted to the world economy and political system. Their curtailed imports will affect economic recovery elsewhere, especially in the industrial countries, whose fastest-growing markets in recent years were the oil-exporting countries. Reduced development efforts - and contraction of the economy - will jeopardize the political stability of a number of exporters. Already, the major industrial countries have organized special efforts to deal with the indebtedness of one oil exporter, Mexico, whose stability and ability to overcome this abrupt change of circumstances is of central foreign policy significance to them.

The changed fortunes of the oil-exporting LDCs will impose costs on the entire financial system - on the commercial banks and public lending institutions. As Kenneth King argues in Chapter 5, whether these costs exceed the benefits stemming from the improved position of the oil-importing developing countries will depend on whether oil prices fall so sharply as to cause an oil-exporting country to default and so bring on a financial crisis which would obstruct world economic recovery. Following the first two oil shocks, funds were recycled from the oil-exporters with the Euromarkets acting as the chief intermediaries. Now the need is to recycle funds in the opposite direction and the official multilateral institutions will probably play a larger role.

Another recycling problem is the curbing of OPEC aid to other LDCs. In 1975, OPEC assistance accounted for about 3% of OPEC GNP and fully one-third of all official assistance. This level has been falling and was only 22% of total international assistance by 1981. Replacing this assistance, which has been concentrated within the Arab world, will be another challenge to the world community. The petroleum industry is often cited as another loser, at least by the bourses of the world. There is no doubt that corporate profits in the oil industry fell dramatically along with the reduction in oil prices. This fall in profitability occurred because the industry's own growth expectations were not fulfilled, perhaps because they were based on the aberrant price increases of 1979-1980. The costs have, however, prompted a rapid adaptation of the oil industry to changed circumstances. Oil companies have drastically reduced, or even eliminated, capital expenditure on synthetic and high-cost fuels. They have pared their non-essential operations and concentrated on development projects with rapid returns. Some smaller, highly geared companies have folded, but the larger integrated companies may well emerge from current circumstances as more efficient enterprises. Indeed, if the analysis earlier in this essay of structural changes in the international petroleum economy is essentially correct, the balance of power in the oil markets will shift increasingly away from producing nations and to the oil companies.

The longer-term balance
While the short-term effects of low oil prices are clearly more beneficial than harmful to the world economy, the longer-term balance is not neatly definable. It depends substantially on the interaction of factors being set in motion today. The dynamics can move in any of several directions.

The future price path is a key variable. For the most part this volume assumes, though it does not predict, price stability. Should the price of oil drop suddenly, demand for petroleum and petroleum products could well exceed the highest levels now envisaged for 1990-5. Investments in new supplies could also fall well below currently anticipated levels owing to uncertainty about the return on capital expenditure. And the impact of dramatically lower prices on the world's financial and commercial structures could be chaotic.

Another aspect of the longer-run balance pertains to actions by governments. Few sectors have been as highly politicized as energy. All governments have in the past considered it legitimate actively to intervene in the energy market. Although the petroleum economy is now more competitive than it was, it is an open question whether governments will permit a fully free and competitive petroleum economy to develop. The principal oil exporters have good reason not to do so. That is why OPEC may well withstand the pressures it is now undergoing. Conversely, the consumer countries might permit domestic prices of petroleum and petroleum products to fall freely, but if they attach importance to conservation, fuel-switching and overall energy security, they will act to prevent it.

Many of the issues relating to the longer-term balance may be summarized by reviewing the energy security questions, and the energy demand and supply responses to lower prices.

A principal danger of lower prices is that a false sense of energy security will lead governments to take no steps to enhance their energy security, and instead actually to dis mantle the instruments now available to deal with it. Indeed, there is a danger that the vulnerability of the economies of the world to a supply disruption may increase.

Efforts to improve energy security were uppermost on the agenda of the Western countries after 1973. The fundamental changes in the structure of the energy sector do not mean that these efforts should be terminated. Rather, as Hanns Maull argues in Chapter 7, it is essential to rethink energy security issues under new circumstances, involving a freer environment with cyclical changes in price.

Petroleum security has involved several strands of policy in the West. It has been based, first, on ensuring that supply lines from exporting countries are as secure from interruption as they reasonably can be; second, on reinforcing 'friendly' governments in the Middle East, through direct assistance, through a network of bilateral trade ties, and through the US Rapid Deployment Force (and potentially, through a future European RDF); third, on measures to deal with a future supply interruption - the establishment of the International Energy Agency's emergency sharing programme and the building of public stocks as a deterrent to an interruption and for use in case one occurred; and, fourth, on the longer-term effort to reduce the importance of energy in the industrial countries' economies (i.e. breaking the linkage between growth in GNP and energy demand), reducing oil's share in overall energy use, and bringing onstream new supplies of conventional and unconventional energy.

This overall Western strategy assumed that the world economy was in transition between an oil-based economy and one in which other fuels would be available in abundance. This central assumption is challenged by the current supply overhang and the recent reductions in prices. The signals that these convey in the market-place may persuade consumers or investors to behave in ways which in the longer run may prove detrimental. While there is little doubt that governments should, in general, build their energy policies on what the market will bear, what role should governments assume if market signals lead to over-consumption and under-investment in new supplies? Longer-term energy security may require governments to intervene to promote conservation and the development of new supplies, both conventional and unconventional.

The area of the energy economy about which analysts know least is the demand response to downward movements in price. Most analysts currently seem confident that a stable price of $29 per barrel will enhance economic activity

23

without reducing the incentives to conserve. But there is no guarantee that the demand response will not be more robust - just as it was stronger and far more rapid when prices were escalating than anyone had predicted. The more price levels fall, the more likely is such a response to develop. If it does, the longer-term balance of costs and benefits will shift, and the industrial countries might find their economies even more vulnerable to another disruption than they were to the last.

Governments will be inclined to undertake actions on the demand side, in response to lower prices, but probably for reasons related less to energy security than to budgets. Governments in consuming countries are likely to see the energy sector more as a source of revenue than as one related to the fundamental welfare of society as a whole. Consumer taxes and tariffs on imports will more likely be tempting devices for revenue enhancement than protection against wrong signals to consumers. Governments are less likely to try to define a floor price for energy security purposes, so as to continue the momentum of the 1970s to conservation and fuel-switching. They may judge the costs of any direct form of such intervention to be greater than the longer-term losses to energy security of a future, price-induced surge in demand.

On the supply side, there are a number of paths which the market could follow as a result of lower prices. Much has been made of the fact that the rate of increase in petroleum reserves outside of OPEC during the past decade has outpaced by far the growth in proved and probable OPEC reserves. But a decline in the future rate of growth is more likely than recent trends would indicate. If the rate of investment slows down, then some OPEC countries will be increasingly well poised to increase substantially their and OPEC's market share, given the much lower costs of developing petroleum resources in the Middle East than elsewhere in the world.

On the other hand, the competition for diminished investment capital among governments should, when combined with lower costs of some exploration and production activities, improve investment terms worldwide and result in an appropriate supply response for conventional fuels. Governments can spur on this supply response by providing fiscal incentives for petroleum investments. The United States government could, for example, take additional steps to promote a supply response outside OPEC by adjusting its own fiscal regime to allow US companies fully to offset exploration costs outside the United States and to credit quasi-tax payments to foreign governments against their United States tax liabilities(10).

Finally, energy security may itself warrant efforts to accelerate the development of alternative fuels. If a diversified fuel mix is a central longer-term goal of energy security, appropriate government intervention should be considered for bio-mass, solar and synthetic fuels.

In the broader context, the long-term outcome will be influenced by how propitiously the short-term benefits and costs occur. The world economic recession has seriously weakened the international trade and financial systems. This is the second year in which international trade has contracted, after thirty years of expansion at 7% annually. The repercussions, particularly on employment in the industrial countries, have prompted an increase in protection. A vicious circle, in which shrinking trade and protection provoke one another, threatens to set in unless world economic activity revives soon. Furthermore, because of adverse trade balances and another feature of the recession, high interest rates, the ability of developing countries to service their debt has deteriorated acutely. An unprecedented number have recently rescheduled their debt and a few have come close to outright default. There is a high risk of an international financial crisis, which would significantly restrict the international banks' capacity to finance world trade and investment.

If the burdens imposed by higher oil prices are not alleviated before the full weight of the burdens imposed by lower oil prices have to be shouldered, the international trade and finance systems could come under intolerable strains. It is important that the US and other industrial economies recover robustly, increasing imports and generating growth in each other's and LDC's exports, before the impact of retrenchment in the oil-exporting countries strikes the world economy. Similarly, the international financial system may be unable to cope with the new debt problems of oil exporters if it is still struggling with the older debt problems of oil importers. The best way to avoid such possibilities may be to enable the multilateral official financial institutions, with the coordinated support of the industrial countries, more actively to assist those oil exporters facing most difficulty in adjusting to lower oil prices.

The Soviet Union
It is, ironically, difficult to discuss the position of the world's largest producer of oil - and its potentially largest producer of gas - under the same general rubrics that are used to

25

analyse the rest of the world. For in central ways the Soviet Union and its allies are unique. Not integrated into the world economy, the Soviet Union has been able to reap a windfall as a price follower of OPEC. Last year it exported almost 1.3 million b/d to the West. These exports ranked the Soviet Union roughly equal to the mean of OPEC countries in terms of market share, and provided almost 60% of its export earnings. In recent years the United States has made the Soviet energy sector a target of its foreign policy, seeking to deprive the Soviet Union of future energy export earnings. Some analysts, particularly in the United States, advocate a very different policy of keeping the USSR energy independent so as to reduce any long-term interests it might have in Middle East energy supplies.

The short-term effects of declining prices on the Soviet economy have been negative, as Jonathan Stern demonstrates in Chapter 4. The drop in world oil prices can cost the Soviet Union as much as $3 billion in 1983, compared with oil export earnings of more than $11 billion in 1981. The protection of this major source of export earnings must be a central goal of Soviet policy. This was evident in the immediate response to the OPEC decision of March 1983 to reduce the marker price to $29: the Soviets dropped their prices even more in an aggressive effort to maintain their market share.

This unexpected action by the Soviet government, at the very time when a reduction in export volumes had been anticipated, is not at all puzzling. The Soviets needed to find a way to redress the lost foreign exchange earnings, and they did so by a forced shift in volumes to the export sector, probably through conservation and fuel-switching, which will have been facilitated by the decline in economic growth. The action also was of potential short-term value in further dividing the NATO allies over how to deal with the Soviet energy sector. And by bolstering exports the Russians created an opportunity to open a dialogue with OPEC over pricing and production levels. This would represent a useful foreign policy overture, since most of the Arab Gulf countries have refused to recognize the Soviet Union or open discussions with it.

The Soviet Union is, however, likely to reduce its oil exports over the decade and to increase substantially its exports of natural gas to Western Europe. It will in the process become a major participant in international gas trade, in fact perhaps the most important single player. Although it will be much more important as a supplier of gas to Western Europe than as a supplier of oil to the West, the

Soviet Union probably will not use this position to exert political influence. In the longer run, the Soviet government will probably allow Western companies to participate in the exploitation of high-cost frontier areas. The purpose will be to accelerate the development of export earnings, and possibly to enjoy the continued secondary benefit of further dividing Western policies towards the USSR. The Soviet Union has been affected by and, in turn, has affected the international political economy as a result of lower prices. But these impacts have provided little more than a fascinating side-show to the main events in the three rings under the big tent. Neither the Soviet Union as a great power, nor the petroleum sector, nor even East/West relations have been, or are likely to be, greatly affected. The main consequences, as Stern explains, are to be felt in the relations between Russia and its dominions in Eastern Europe.

The overall balance
There can be little doubt that there have been continuing changes in the structure of the international petroleum economy for the past thirty years. Each of the regimes which have controlled the petroleum sector appears to have carried within it the seeds of its own transformation. The OPEC-dominated energy economy of the 1970s in this sense helped to breed the more competitive environment of the 1980s. It seems that this would have been the case, although the timing would have been different, even had the price escalations of 1979-81 not been so steep. Given the pace of conservation and fuel-switching, the political structures of the energy economy could not support $34 per barrel. The price decrease was probably inevitable.

As this essay, and most of the others which follow it, posits, the short-term benefits of an oil price reduction to a stagnating world economy which has experienced a steep decline in productive activity far exceed the costs. The benefits are diffused throughout most of the world economy. The costs are concentrated in the oil-exporting countries. The longer-term balance is less clear. In part this is because where one is going depends on - and is less important than - how one gets there, a question intentionally avoided by these essays. There could be, however, a critical difference between a world energy economy based on stable oil prices for an extended period of time, and fluctuating prices. If OPEC is unable on its own, or in cooperation with other producing/exporting countries, to stabilize prices, the result may well be much greater price variability - rapid changes in price reflecting changes in demand. Extreme fluctuations in prices could have a negative impact on virtually every area touched by the energy sector, but especially on longer-term investments, which would be greatly discouraged. Yet the more competitive environment, which seems ineluctably to be emerging, will have much less price rigidity than the one dominated by OPEC.

Whether the evolution of the petroleum sector will be smooth or bumpy, the emerging international investment order will be much more open to private company investments than that of the late 1960s and 1970s. It seems that competition among companies for access to secure supplies, which characterized the investment environment in the 1970s, is being replaced by a new environment, characterized more by competiton among governments for investment capital. A major challenge to the parties concerned will be to create among private companies, local companies and host governments a contractual relationship which will be more equitable than those of the past and so better able to withstand the vicissitudes of demand.

Other changes could either reinforce or dampen price variability. Change is likely in inventory holdings. There was an enormous run-up in inventories between late 1978 and mid-1980, and a rundown ever since. Some have argued that in the future, because of the growth of new institutions such as the expanded spot market and the futures market, and because of changes in companies' relation ships with customers, stocks will be much less important and too costly for companies to maintain at high levels. The reduction in company and consumer stocks, which many regard as inevitable, should also result in greater seasonal swings in demand on OPEC than has been the case(11). If seasonal shifts in demand become enormous, they could result in larger price variations not only for petroleum, but also for tanker rates.

Perhaps working in the other direction is the development of a futures market. A slack market will create opportunities for the development of a futures market in crude oil and production products. A futures market has already developed internationally in some petroleum products, specifically in home heating oil and gasoline, and is now beginning in crude oil. This development is almost an inevitable result of the growth in the number of national oil companies, who find it in their interest to trade futures in crude in order to assure themselves of an income stream for planning purposes.

If the current glut persists, we can expect the national oil companies of countries such as Mexico, Norway and the

United Kingdom to want to hedge and reduce the uncertain ties associated with their income projections. On the customer side, we can expect a number of public and private institutions to want to buy crude for future delivery, just as they now buy resid, the prime motivation being relative certainty with respect to expenditure. A slack oil market would also make a futures market attractive to a number of marginal exporting developing countries whose most important goal would be stable income on which to base economic plans for the domestic economy. No better means exists to ensure them a steady stream of income than dealing in futures.

Changes in the structure of companies work in the same direction. With governments having more control over resources, and with a long-term supply overhang, the oil companies have much less reason to be concerned with access to supplies than they did in the past. They have discovered the profitability, and for some the necessity, of developing oil-trading operations.

In short, the bases for an institutionalized crude oil futures market exist. It is an open question, however, whether such a market will smooth spot price fluctuations, or whether the operations of speculators will exaggerate them. At a minimum, it would reinforce the trends which appear increasingly to deprive OPEC of its ability to administer world oil prices.

Some OPEC countries understand this and harbour hopes of a dialogue with the major oil-consuming countries. They assume that, on the one hand, both oil-exporting and oil-importing countries will have an interest in preventing the market-place from replacing entirely an administered pricing regime; and, on the other hand, that in the future, OPEC will be unable to play the role of price-maker. Rather, joint efforts will be required, at least to maintain a floor price.

Proposals for an international producer/consumer dialogue have been put forward regularly since 1973. They have never got off the ground for any of a number of reasons. Most often, the consuming countries were too obviously the 'demandeurs' and their bargaining power was too limited. Internal disagreements on both sides made it almost impossible for coherent discussion to take place. And, there were those on the consuming country side who almost always convincingly argued that a dialogue was pointless when no one could impose a ceiling price in a tight market-place.

A dialogue need not, however, result in, or even aim to establish, a full oil commodity pact. A narrower forum than

OPEC's thirteen members and the International Energy Agency's twenty-one could well meet to discuss matters of common concern. They could try to develop a better understanding of actions that might be in their mutual interests, and of actions to be avoided because they would cancel each other out. In the current weak market-place, now may be the most propitious time to launch a dialogue between OPEC and the IEA. Governments on both sides might well have good reasons to want to avoid a drop in the floor price of oil, as well as to avoid rapid price movements. Ironically, if political conditions now seem ripe for such a dialogue, the underlying structural changes in the petroleum market may be so great that such a dialogue could be futile. The market may now be out of the control of a few powerful participants and increasingly subject to the interplay between demand and supply and the participation of multiple, weaker participants.

Notes

1. See, in particular, Robert Doliner, 'The OPEC Tax Cut of 1983: Economic Recovery and the Decline in Oil Prices', Cambridge Energy Research Associates (April, 1983).
2. An excellent example of this mode of thought can be found in Joseph S. Nye, 'Energy and Security', in David A. Deese and Joseph S. Nye, eds., Energy and Security (Cambridge, MA, Ballinger, 1981), pp.3-22.
3. For solid discussions of the cyclical aspects of the oil market, see Øystein Noreng, 'World Oil Market Prospects in the 1980s in the Context of Three Different Perspectives' (pp.89-102), and Robert Mabro, 'OPEC's Future Pricing Role May Be at Stake' (pp.147-54), in Miguel S. Wionczek, ed., World Hydrocarbon Markets (Oxford, Pergamon Press, 1983).
4. A brief and succinct overview is John H. Lichtblau, 'The World Petroleum Outlook' (New York, PIRINC, 23 April 1982).
5. International Energy Agency, World Energy Outlook (Paris, OECD, 1982), p.69.
6. Edwin A. Deagle, Jr., The Future of the International Oil Market: A Report Prepared for the Study Group on Energy and the World Economy (New York, Group of Thirty, March 1983), pp.29-31.
7. Bijan Mossavar-Rahmani has recently argued that for OPEC to play the balancer requires these enormous production shifts because of what he calls 'the OPEC

multiplier'. Since OPEC countries are the marginal suppliers, 'a small increase in world oil demand results in a disproportionately large percentage increase in demand for OPEC oil, and a small decrease in world oil demand results in a disproportionately large decrease in OPEC oil'. 'The OPEC Multiplier: Rebound of the Oil Exporters?', Cambridge Energy Research Associates (November, 1982), p.4.

8. This view of Saudi motivations is largely informed by William B. Quandt, Saudi Arabia in the 1980s: Foreign Policy, Security and Oil (Washington, DC, Brookings Institution, 1981).

9. World Financial Markets (New York, Morgan Guaranty Trust Company of New York, April 1983), pp.7-9.

10. This is recommended in Third World Petroleum Development (Washington, DC, National Petroleum Council, 1983).

11. See Philip K. Verleger, Jr., 'The Economic Implications of Structural Change in the Petroleum Industry', Energy (New York, Drexel, Burnham, Lambert, February 1983).

31

2 Oil-exporting Countries

Albert Bressand, Catherine Distler and Ghassane Salame*

Compared with other economic problems, energy issues tend to look clear-cut. Oil price changes can be measured much less ambiguously than, say, monetary aggregates, and their economic impact lends itself to misleadingly simple quantification. The temptation is to describe the recent decline in oil prices as the straightforward counter-equivalent of previous price rises. To consumers considering the impact on exporting countries, the notion that 'lower' oil prices simply undo what 'higher' oil prices did in the past may be particularly appealing. This 'wishful thinking' approach to the world energy scene cannot really capture the essence of the oil price impact on the national and international economy.

First, 'lower prices', as the comparative adjective suggests, cannot be treated by themselves (indeed, they are anything but 'low prices'). They are, by definition, those prices that follow a 'higher' price period. As we shall see, their impact cannot be isolated from this context. What is actually under discussion is not lower prices but upward and downward movements in oil prices, considered as a single phenomenon.

Second, we know very well in the case of the consumer countries that oil price increases were only one element of a more complex economic picture. The impact of 'oil shocks' depended decisively on other key developments, such as trends in world inflation, incipient disorder in the world monetary system, and changing patterns of industrial competitiveness - all of which preceded, interacted with and influenced energy trends. For similar reasons, one should beware of analysing the economic situation of oil-exporting countries in the narrow terms of reduced oil revenues. A

---

* The authors want to thank Murielle Delaporte, a research assistant at IFRI, for her help in this project.

nation, even an oil-exporting one, is not an oil company. The impact of oil price movements on its economy cannot be assessed independently from the other trends at work. Of course, lower oil prices have an important mechanical impact on such critical areas as the current account, government revenues and indebtedness. Yet it is worth reflecting on the striking similarities which Brazil's, Argentina's and Mexico's economic situations exhibit at present, although Brazil is a major net oil importer, whereas Argentina is just about self-sufficient in energy and Mexico is a leading oil exporter. Some of the similarities (which of course coexist with major differences) are less surprising in the light of the point already made about the importance of price fluctuations (which all countries have experienced) rather than a 'high' or 'low' price per se.

Although we cannot here present a detailed view of global international economic interactions(1), in assessing the impact of 'lower oil prices' on the exporting countries we will strive to convey a taste of the importance of global inter-dependence - both within and across countries.

The case of Mexico is probably the best illustration of the need to take a broad view of the impact of oil prices. Many of the country's present difficulties are related to funda-mental demographic and economic problems as well as to the perverse impact of the oil boom, with softening prices being only one complicating factor.

At the other end of the spectrum, for Saudi Arabia and other countries of the Gulf financial surpluses provide a buffer between the national economy and the international energy system from which the money flows. Nonetheless, the geographical situation of the region, and notably the Iran/Iraq war, is a powerful influence in shaping attitudes, expectat-ions and reactions to the present oil price trends.

Between these two types are countries such as Nigeria and Venezuela where the impact of lower oil prices is neither buffered by the accumulated wealth of the Gulf nor obscured by the complexity of an advanced economy such as Mexico.

Mexico
Of all the oil-exporting countries, Mexico provides the most telling example of the ambivalence of oil and of its potential to wreak havoc on an economy even before the bonanza is over. The present depth of Mexican difficulties - in which oil is a major ingredient although far from the only one - is the

more remarkable as Mexico had always professed to be fully aware of the dangers of oil dependency and seemed to be well-placed, politically and economically, to avert them. A basic tenet of all Mexican presidents has been to adjust prudently the flow of oil to the long-term needs of the country. Yet the ceilings imposed on production and exports in the late 1970s kept creeping up. The often proclaimed will to refuse to allow market forces to decide production levels played a useful short-term role in strengthening the government's hand in its relations with present and potential buyers. But, over the medium term, one may doubt whether the evolution of production differed substantially from what a pure market approach would have brought about. As reserves were constantly revalued, production climbed from 0.9 million b/d in 1977 to 3 million b/d in 1982, when Mexico was the third largest producer in the non-communist world.

As in other oil- and gas-exporting countries (one is reminded for instance of Algeria), the building up of a strong energy base was achieved at no small cost to the economy. The national oil company, Pemex, absorbed a full quarter of government budgets during the past three years. A predominant share of investment went into the petroleum and petrochemicals sectors. Supposedly an unlimited provider of foreign exchange, oil also became a major source of indebtedness and dependency. This excessive development of an oil economy within the economy was reflected in the soaring public-sector deficit, in financing needs, and in inflation. Temporary relief was afforded by the second oil shock, which turned the rapid rise in oil production into a massive expansion of export revenues, from $1 billion in 1977 to $15 billion (75% of total export earnings) in 1982. Despite enormous waste, the period between 1978 and 1981 saw the creation of 2.8 million jobs, a growth rate of 8% (against 3.2% in 1975-8), and vigorous progress in industrialization.

A score of internal political, economic and demographic factors combined to bring about a situation in which economic and financial prudence was disregarded, and the Mexican oil boom got totally out of control at both the management and the political level. The first policy mistake was to dismiss the early warnings of the markets. Not that Jorge Dias Serrano, the then director of Pemex, had not read the writing on the wall: aware that Mexico's stubborn refusal to follow the tide of softening prices was substantially reducing its market share, he eventually decided in June 1981 to slash Mexican prices by $4. In a country where oil prices had become an essential symbol of economic nationalism and with a presidential election campaign in the offing, the price adjustment was soon reversed. Predictable consequences followed, at a cost to the Mexican treasury of $5-$7 billion in lost sales. In due course, the price rebate had to be reinstated, but the Mexican propensity to turn oil policy to domestic political purposes had been vividly demonstrated. The financial counterpart of this neglect of fundamental trends in the oil market was a quite extraordinary explosion of short-term borrowing to make up for lost reveue. Resistance to market realities was also evident in an exchange rate policy which maintained the parity of the peso against the dollar despite its substantial overvaluation.

The moment of truth, however, was approaching. Although so-called 'lower oil prices' were instrumental in bringing it about, they were only an accelerating factor. By themselves, they could not have produced a shock in any way comparable to the one Mexico is now going through. In addition, the impact of a decline in oil prices can be offset by changes in some of the other elements that have contributed to the present disequilibria. It should be noted, for example, that a decline of one dollar in the price of the 1.5 million barrels of oil which Mexico now exports has almost the same impact on the current account balance as a 1% rise in interest rates (i.e. $550 million versus $500 million). When these two factors work in the same direction, as they did in 1981-2, their impact for a net borrower like Mexico is cumulative. When they work in opposite directions (as they did in 1982 and early 1983) lower interest rates can cancel the impact of lower oil prices.

There are in fact several ways in which 'high' oil prices, rather than 'low' ones, are to blame for Mexico's failure to protect its market share in late 1981: they provoked tactical mistakes; and over the long term they led to a wasteful growth process which disregarded basic development needs. In any case, the bubble of excessive expectations brought about by the boom has now burst.

To careful observers, the first signs of impending disaster were apparent as early as 1979 as the net flow of money to Mexico began to recede. The huge borrowing in which the country continued to indulge, abetted by international banks still eager to lend to it, served only to service and refinance an already unreasonable debt. Yet it was not until the crisis of August 1982 that the Mexican establishment realized that the problem had grown to uncontrollable proportions, with a total external debt of $80 to $85 billion, of which about $69 billion was owed by the public sector.

A rescue operation was mounted by the Bank for International Settlements, the United States (for which Mexico has important foreign policy significance) and, at a later stage, the IMF. Oil exports played a role in the American component of the package, in the form of a $1 billion advance payment for increased purchases of oil for the Strategic Petroleum Reserve, which included an agreement on prices out of keeping with the Reagan Administration's free-market philosophy: a $35 ceiling and a $25 floor were written into the deal.

Oil revenues (which are intimately related to oil prices but in a complex fashion that incorporates competition for market shares) will of course also play a major role in meeting the short-term financial objectives. In 1983, the Mexican government - according to a document released in February 1983 - expects export revenue of $21.9 billion, of which $15.9 billion will be from oil exports. Lower oil prices would make this objective difficult to fulfil, although, as we have seen, favourable developments in interest rates would compensate for oil income shortfalls. But, as the analysis of Mexican problems suggests, oil price and export developments will be only one important, yet by no means overriding, element in the success or failure of the present strategy. If they help to convince Mexican politicians, officials and public opinion of the urgency of adopting an overall development strategy in which oil is but one component, then 'lower' oil prices will be as beneficial to Mexico as the oil boom was detrimental. Mexico will have also to take careful stock of its role in the world energy economy and in particular decide whether to pursue further its recent interchanges with OPEC.

Nigeria

In recent years non-OPEC exporters consistently followed a market-oriented price policy: they undercut OPEC prices each time the market weakened but tried to take advantage of the market during the booms. Since the glut began, the non-Arab members of OPEC have had difficulty in finding customers each time non-OPEC exporters made price cuts which they were unable to match. Nigeria's vulnerability to North Sea prices was demonstrated throughout the past three years and led it to decide in 1983 to undercut BNOC prices. Reduced export revenues have aggravated debt problems. Much more clearly than in the case of Mexico they have been a major factor in these countries' overall economic situation.

The case of Nigeria offers an eloquent example.

Government oil revenues in Nigeria declined from $23.4 billion in 1980 to $16.7 billion in 1981, when, despite requests from some companies, it refused to cut oil prices by $5. Owing to its geographical location and the quality of its crude, Nigeria is greatly influenced by North Sea price and production trends. The government has become increasingly aware of this vulnerability and, after the 1981 sequence was repeated in 1982 and at the beginning of 1983, it decided to undercut North Sea prices in February 1983, so contributing to the eventual outcome of the London Agreement on prices and quotas.

Nigeria did not have any real choice. Substantial foreign reserves and a very low level of international borrowing had allowed it to maintain import levels during the arm-twisting period of 1981, but by April 1982 the government had to enact major import restrictions in order to cut the import bill by one-third. The problem worsened throughout 1982 as Nigeria failed to meet its target of keeping imports below 800 million naira a month (against a previous level of N1200 per month) and as arrears in trade payments increased to $5 billion. In January 1983 further restrictions were introduced, including two- and threefold increases in tariffs and duties (in some cases to a level of 100%), extension of the list of goods requiring import licences, and prohibition of some luxury items. The aim was to reduce imports to N600 million a month and to protect local manufacturers. At the same time the Central Bank was trying to borrow $2 billion to reduce the trade payments backlog.

There is reason to doubt whether Nigeria's current policy will succeed and hence whether the objectives set in the new government budget will be achieved. The government is feeling constrained by the prospect of national elections, which are to take place in August 1983 for the first time since the return to civilian government in 1979, following thirteen years of military rule. Moreover, the recent austerity measures have resulted in growing unemployment, a 25% increase in food prices, and widespread discontent; while output, which is estimated to have fallen by 7% in the past two years, will continue to be affected by lower oil production and reduced government spending. The 3% growth forecast in the budget now looks a very ambitious target.

At present oil prices, the level of oil production required to meet the 1983 budget requirements is 1.3 million b/d, the exact quota allowed by the London Agreement. To raise its production to this ceiling, Nigeria will have to ensure that the price differential between Bonny light crude oil and Arabian light crude oil works in its favour. This explains the stubborn efforts made during the London meeting by Mallam Dikko, the oil adviser to President Shagari, to hold this differential to only one dollar in spite of Sheikh Yamani's determination to set it at 2.5 or 3, which would have more closely reflected the differences in location and quality.

Despite the low level of Nigeria's debt ($6 billion) and its debt-service ratio of 7%, there is concern among bankers about the quality of external debt management and the liquidity problem created by the oil glut. They are very reluctant to undertake a rescheduling of Nigerian debt until Nigeria agrees to an IMF-sponsored adjustment policy. Yet the Nigerian government is less than enthusiastic about the standard IMF package of a devaluation and the elimination of subsidies to consumers just a few months before elections. The present fragile political consensus has been carefully nurtured through skilful distribution of the oil wealth. The government is concerned that less manna from heaven might prompt the revival of regionalism among the three main tribal groups of the country.

During the last quarter of 1982, violent religious riots took place in the three main towns of the north, which had already seen similar events two years earlier. The many Hausa-speaking Muslims who had migrated to this region from Chad, Niger and Cameroon were believed to be responsible for the spread of Islamic Fundamentalism which inspired the rioters. In the south, especially near Lagos, growing unemployment, resulting from cutbacks in investment plans and lower government spending, exacerbated the latent xenophobia engendered by the presence of more than one million illegal Ghanaian immigrants.

Thus the order given in January that aliens without valid papers must leave Nigeria was a pre-electoral measure on two levels. However, this exodus will have scant effect on unemployment, since unskilled Nigerians can hardly replace skilled Ghanaian workers. The situation is compounded by import restictions which have resulted in a raw materials shortage, so that parts of industry have had to cut back production and lay off workers.

After swallowing two austerity budgets in a row, President Shagari has to find a way to deal with short-term liquidity problems and at the same time persuade Nigerians that hopes of building the most prosperous and powerful country in black Africa can be fulfilled.

Venezuela

Venezuela, one of the six founding members of OPEC, has pursued a very clear price and production policy since the second oil shock: it has favoured higher prices because they make economic the development of the costly heavy oil of the Orinoco tar belt, and because of the country's large debt it is very sensitive to production cuts needed in the cause of OPEC solidarity.

Both in the first agreement - on an overall production ceiling in March 1982 - and in the London Agreement, Venezuela was one of the few countries to have its quota set below the level of previous production. So, in July 1982, after the meeting in Geneva had failed to find a solution to the problems posed by Iran's decision to produce 1 million b/d over its quota and to undercut OPEC prices by $3, Venezuela increased its production so as to restore its market share, arguing that the March 1982 agreement was no longer valid. In March 1983, despite the quota agreement, Venezuela maintained production at the same level until the end of the month, so benefiting from exports of about 250,000 b/d above its quota. The explanation offered was that, for technical reasons, it was extremely difficult to reduce production at short notice.

The London Agreement on production and prices implied a reduction of $3 billion in Venezuelan oil export revenue in 1983, from $15 billion in 1982. Venezuela's reluctance to accept a price cut in current dollars was very strong in March 1983, as it had been in summer 1981. Because Venezuela buys a much larger proportion of its imports from the United States than do other OPEC countries, at a time when the dollar is strengthening it is hit harder than the others by a decline in its dollar income from oil exports.

Like many Latin American countries, Venezuela has a large debt: $30 billion. Its long-term position is far better than Mexico's but it failed to prevent short-term debt from piling up ($13 billion are due in 1983, of which $10 billion are short-term debt). In fact, the perils of short-term borrowing were not lost on the Venezuelans. In 1981, Congress passed the Refinancing Act, authorizing the government to transform more than $12 billion of short-term debt into medium- and long-term debt. However, the committee that was set up to handle debt management lacked the power to implement its responsibilities. Furthermore, foreign banks became unwilling to roll over Venezuela's short-term debt as the Euromarkets began to be more cautious about lending to Latin America.

In order to increase its international reserves, the Central Bank took control of the financial assets of Petroleos de Venezuela, the state oil company, and of the Venezuelan Investment Fund ($7 billion). In response to a steady capital flight at the end of 1982, the government introduced foreign exchange controls, and in February 1983 it established a three-tier exchange rate for the bolivar, in the first devaluation against the dollar for twenty years. Although maintaining the interest payments on all loans, Venezuela delayed any repayment of principal to 1 July, pending a rescheduling of its short-term debt.

The growing worries of international bankers stem from the reluctance of the Venezuelan government to initiate an adjustment policy: despite a 30% reduction in revenues, public expenditure has been cut by only 2.5% and the heavily subsidized domestic energy prices have not been raised. As in Mexico in 1982, the government is paralysed by the forthcoming presidential election (December 1983). Consequently it is unwilling to seek an IMF loan, although the medium-term outlook is bleak. The oil glut seems likely to last for some time, and, while it does, no significant increase in oil export revenues can be expected. Yet they account for 90% of total export revenues in a trade balance which has been estimated to be in deficit by $2 billion.

Financial difficulties and uncertainty about the prospects for oil have already caused some longer-term projects to be abandoned. The construction of the Lagoven refinery, which would have had an input capacity of 170,000 b/d of heavy oil from 1988, has been cancelled. Moreover, development of the Orinoco tar belt, whose oil was to secure Venezuela's future when existing sources of oil were exhausted towards the turn of the century, has been postponed, perhaps indefinitely.

The Gulf producers

In the Gulf area, the most outstanding factor is clearly the coincidence of the downturn in the oil market and the Iran/Iraq war. These two developments had the effect of depriving the two belligerents of a major part of their oil revenues and of their international financial assets.

Paradoxically, from a strictly financial point of view, the status quo is probably the best situation for the GCC producers(2). The closing of the Iraqi terminals on the Gulf and of the Banias and Tripoli pipeline substantially restricts

Iraq's exports. The war is thus allowing the other Gulf producers a larger share of the market than they would otherwise have had.

If the war ends with a formal agreement between the two belligerents, the GCC producers will be obliged to accept a substantial increase in Iraqi (and perhaps Iranian) oil production, and a commensurate lowering of their own. Moreover, they may have to cement this agreement by paying war reparations to Iran, though they could escape this obligation if the war, instead of coming to a formal end, progressively dies down after new but unsuccessful Iranian attacks. An undeclared, albeit effective, truce could emerge, opening the way to repair the Iraqi and Iranian oil installations. After the losses that they have suffered, both (especially Iraq) will want to increase their production in the shortest possible time. This could mean 2 to 2.5 million b/d for each of the two belligerents. Given the political pressures both of them could exert, the GCC countries will probably accept this increase and the consequent cutback in their own production. The initial economic effect on the GCC countries will be that they have to rely for revenue more on their foreign reserves and less on their oil exports; later they will have to impose strict limits on government spending and on costly development projects.

Another possible (but less likely) outcome is an Iranian triumph in the war. This would affect the stability and finances of the GCC countries more than their oil production. They might rush to help Iraq by paying, among other things, its armaments bills. Another option could be to negotiate directly with the Iranians, as was often suggested in June 1982 at the height of the Iranian offensive. This would mean paying war reparations to Iran and accepting the level Teheran chose for its oil production.

Saudi Arabia
The main effect of the London Agreement was obviously the formalizing of Saudi Arabia's role of swing producer, with the hypothetical ability to fill the gap between the 12.5 million b/d allocated to the twelve other OPEC members and the overall demand for OPEC oil. But the swing now has a downward bias: with demand of 15 to 16 million b/d for OPEC oil, the Saudis are producing around 4 million b/d - i.e. the balance plus the unused part of the quota production of other members. In the highly unlikely event of an abrupt rise in demand, Saudi Arabia would probably be unable to resist the pressures for a new agreement on production ceilings which

would increase the quotas of the financially hard-pressed countries(3). Hence it is improbable that Saudi production will go much beyond 4 to 5 million b/d within the next two to three years or even longer.

The Saudi budget for 1983-4 does not incorporate the present substantial drop in the kingdom's revenues. Projected revenues are about $65 billion: realistic estimates put the actual level at 50% to 60% of this figure. If Saudi Arabia is able to export an average of 4.5 million b/d during 1983-4, and if the price holds at $29 per barrel, its revenues will not exceed $45 billion. But the odds are that Saudi exports will be below this average. Because of the fall in oil output, NGL (natural gas liquids) exports are not likely to generate more than $3 to $4 billion of additional revenue. Investment income from Saudi Arabia's official assets of $140 to $150 billion will probably not exceed $12 to $15 billion.

In the short term, Saudi Arabia will therefore have to take a tougher look at its budgetary objectives. If the Saudi government sticks to its planned spending ($75.6 billion), it will have to draw on its foreign assets more heavily than its announced intentions indicate. The Saudi leaders could choose to reduce government spending much more drastically. This would slow down economic growth and, possibly, lead to social and political discontent. Saudi Arabia has not yet had to face this choice.

Saudi Arabia seems most unlikely to return to its sky-rocketing earnings of 1980-1. Even if there is an upturn in oil production in 1985 or 1986, the Saudi share is not very likely to go beyond 5 or 6 million b/d, especially if the Iran/Iraq war has ended by then.

These changed circumstances will certainly be reflected in the fourth Development Plan (1985-90). But there is no reason to suppose that the current plan will be affected during its remaining two years, since it was conceived before the second oil shock when the price was at $17 a barrel. So far the Saudis have made no fundamental changes. What they have done and will probably do again next year is to make a general reduction in all the budgetary allocations except defence. This will certainly affect all categories of construction, especially large new hospitals, schools and roads. The slowdown will also affect the petrochemical industry, but not before 1985-6 when the projects now being completed will begin production. As for oil production itself, plans to build a pipeline from Kuwait to Oman will probably be discarded. The pace of exploration is being maintained. There are strong signs of a new preference for non-associated gas, for which a series of exploration contracts are expected to be awarded during the next few months.

Kuwait
With $75 to $80 billion of foreign investment, earning $8 to $10 billion of annual revenue, Kuwait is in an enviable position. Like Iran, this emirate adopted before the downturn of the oil market a policy of conservation which greatly eased the impact on public opinion of lower oil revenues. The planned deficit in the budget should be viewed in this context, which also explains why changes in the oil market will have no substantial direct effects on the economy.

Probably more worrisome are the economic implications of the Iran/Iraq war: owing to Iraq's financial problems, exports to that country are declining daily. Within a general climate of insecurity, financial confidence is in a particularly fragile state following the Al-Mannakh scandal, which culminated in the collapse of the stock market. The government seems to be hesitant in its handling of the whole question: unable to act as guarantor to make good the large amounts of postdated cheques, but equally fearful, if the law is strictly applied, of a long chain of bankruptcies. This climate has affected the banking sector, which is now growing at a much slower pace. A parallel speculation took place in the real estate sector, and the government was dismayed to discover, here too, a series of transactions based on postdated cheques.

Kuwait is, of course, also much concerned by the political repercussions of the war that is taking place on its doorstep. There is the permanent fear that it will spill over. The Kuwaitis have not forgotten the three air attacks conducted in 1981 against targets in their territory, one of them against the oil installations at Umm al-Aich. Their geopolitical situation makes them highly susceptible to pressures and threats from their strong neighbours. Kuwait has had to contribute to the Iraqi war effort and probably will have, later, to pay war reparations to Iran. A further cause for worry is the possibility that a complete collapse of the Reagan and Fez peace plans will lead to disturbances in Kuwait among Palestinian and other expatriates. The combination of these factors, together with the near absence of investment opportunities in Kuwait itself, is inducing both the government and the private sector to look for foreign opportunities.

Oman
Although not directly affected by war, Oman has been

devoting a large part of its budget to military expenditure. The sultanate will probably have to slow down its spending and to tap the international capital market for a loan. It is now obvious that the budgetary allocations for 1983 were over-optimistic. The government was planning to spend some $4 million more than in 1982. The revenues were planned to come mainly from oil exports ($3.4 billion out of total oil export earnings of $42 billion) with a deficit of $0.6 billion. Oman's optimism apparently stemmed from the fact that it was able to sell more of its oil despite a sluggish market. But the sultanate, though not a member of OPEC, will now have to follow the trend set by OPEC producers. Oman can count on only limited revenue from foreign aid (estimated at $35 million in the budget) and from its modest foreign assest ($1.5 to $2 billion). If it seeks to borrow, the odds are that the sultanate's relatively promising economic situation will encourage banks to answer positively.

Iraq
Iraq has problems caused by the combination of the war and the downturn in the oil market. The Iraqi leaders have deferred as long as they could any hard choice between guns and butter. The feeling in fact was that butter was needed at home if the sound of guns was not to put Sadam Hussein's regime in jeopardy. Thus, imports rose to $18.4 billion in the first half of 1981, compared with $13.5 billion for the corresponding period of 1980. In the first year of the war, the development budget was increased by 28% to more than $23 billion dollars! Construction projects in Baghdad alone accounted for more than $8 billion.

But, with oil exports now averaging only 650,000 b/d as the war goes on much longer than ever anticipated, the strategy of fighting simultaneously on the military and economic fronts cannot be sustained. After the Iranian successes of autumn 1981 and spring 1982, Iraq had no option but to slow down drastically its development projects and spending in order to free as many resources as possible for military purchases. A moratorium on new contracts was declared in December 1981. Austerity became the norm through 1982, when aid from the GCC countries was suspended. Iraq has had difficulties in paying foreign contractors and has asked companies to arrange their own sources of credit. Some items are in short supply, and the price of many has risen steeply.

Iraq has had a $500 million loan from the Euromarket and will have to return to the market for further funds. The banks may respond favourably in view of Iraq's good economic prospects and fierce military resistance. Baghdad is seeking credit mainly for new military contracts. The Development Plan has already had to be shelved: the $26 billion planned to be spent during 1982 were not available.

Iran

Iran is the only gainer among oil-exporting countries after more than two years of oil glut and the negotiation of the London Agreement. Its successes have occurred both in the market-place and at a political level, inside the Gulf area and within OPEC.

Yet, in 1981, nobody could have foreseen such an outcome. Owing to declining oil demand and very aggressive price competition, Iran's situation on the oil market had deteriorated rapidly in 1980-1. The oil revenues fell significantly below government expectations at the very time when Iran needed foreign exchange to sustain imports vital for its population (foodstuffs and medicine) and for its war effort. There were two ways in which it could increase its share of a shrinking oil market: by arranging new barter deals with East European or developing countries and by offering substantial discounts to attract cash buyers.

In spring 1982, when the country's financial reserves were quite exhausted, Iran initiated a policy of high oil exports at any price. Its oil price was set $4 below the OPEC official price and $7 below the price it had been selling at two years before. Iranian oil production climbed to 2 million b/d (800,000 b/d above the ceiling set under the March 1982 agreement) during the second quarter of 1982, then to 2.2 and 2.7 during the third and fourth. Oil revenues were sufficient not only to cover import requirements, but also to enable foreign exchange reserves - of around $1 billion a month - to accumulate. The main task was then to ligitimize Iran's de facto position as the second largest producer in OPEC.

Price discounts had exposed Iran to strong criticism from the other oil exporters, who were worried about the threat to OPEC's price structure, but it was bolstered by its improved position in the war since the offensive of July. Moreover, Saudi Arabia and other GCC countries were worried that Iran's improved earning power could help it to spread the Islamic revolution all over the Gulf.

At the London meeting, Iran reached an enviable result: it formally re-established its position as the second producer in OPEC, which it had ceded after the 1979 revolution, and it secured a production ceiling which is double its previous one

(2.4 million b/d instead of 1.2 million b/d) and sufficient to meet its short-term import needs.

But many of Iran's longer-term problems remain unresolved. Despite promises of the new Islamic government to build an economy self-sufficient in agriculture and industry and less dependent on oil exports and manufactured imports, the only success of the post-revolutionary government has been to change the law governing ownership of economic resources (Islamicization of the economy). The Iranian economy has been suffering heavily since the beginning of the Iran/Iraq war, and losses are estimated at $90 billion. By far the most decisive factor for the economy will be the course of the war and the possible payment of damages by other Gulf countries (Saudi Arabia, Kuwait). Whatever the result of the fighting, however, Iran will need a higher level of oil production to rebuild its economy.

Conclusion
The oil exporters' international political standing will reflect the change in their economic fortunes. There will be a general decline in OPEC's influence in the international system. However, this trend will be much more significant in the case of Arab producers who made use of the 'oil weapon' in their dealings with the West and of the 'oil money weapon' in their relations with the developing countries of Africa and Asia. This decline will obviously affect producers such as Libya and Iraq, Kuwait and Algeria. Particularly within the Arab world such a decline is unavoidable, since large amounts of aid were almost the only tool used by the oil exporters to exert pressure or to obtain political results. The single Arab country which could be most severely affected by this downturn is Saudi Arabia. The Middle East is indeed witnessing the end of what Muhammad Hassanein Heikal once called 'the Saudi era'.

There has probably been too much rejoicing in the West at these developments. Suggestions have been made that Western Europe need no longer worry about its relations with the Arab world, nor issue - without much conviction - communiques like the Venice one. But this is a very shortsighted view. Western (and especially US) influence in the Middle East, unlike that of the Soviet Union, grew steadily during the past decade as a result, at least partially, of the leverage acquired by countries like Saudi Arabia on the more radical Arab countries. Hence the decline in Western influence entails a decline in Western influence, which has been evident in the recent ascendance of the Soviet Union in both Syria and Iraq, and in the failure of the Reagan Plan. It is in any case unlikely that the Arabs will put aside the Arab/Israeli conflict just because they are no longer able to use the 'oil weapon'; they will, more likely, look to other means at their disposal, including a general rapprochement with the Soviet Union. This trend could be accelerated by stronger public pressure on Arab governments.

In the long run, Western dependence on OPEC, and especially Middle East, oil is unavoidable. The Middle East producers account for three-fifths of all proven reserves outside the communist area. From the producers' side, this clearly means that if they can survive beyond the present crisis - and the four GCC countries in OPEC easily can - they will, sooner or later (possibly around 1986), achieve a better share of the market. This is especially the case for Saudi Arabia, which has at least 160 billion of barrels in proven reserves, Kuwait (64 billion) and the UAE (32 billion). Political influence could stem from future needs as well as from present ones.

Notes
1. See Albert Bressand, 'Mastering the "World Economy"', Foreign Affairs, Spring 1983.
2. The Gulf Cooperation Council was created on 25 March 1981. Its members are Qatar, Bahrain, Oman, Kuwait, the United Arab Emirates and Saudi Arabia.
3. Iran's ability to double its quota between the April 1982 and March 1983 agreements can at least partially be explained by the improvement of its military position during this period.

3 Oil-importing Developing Countries

David Pearce*

Adjustments to high oil prices

Most oil-importing developing nations sustained a heavy burden of adjustment to the oil price rises of 1973-4 and 1979. Some, like India and China, remained relatively unaffected owing to high levels of self-sufficiency and high investment ratios based on domestic savings. For most, however, the only mechanism of adjustment was to reduce oil imports, increase foreign borrowing and sustain reduced levels of economic activity. Thus, whereas China and India actually increased their economic growth rates after 1973 (from 4.7% p.a. to 5.3% p.a. for China when comparing 1960-73 with 1973-80, and from 3.5 to 3.8% for India), low-income oil importers sustained absolute GDP reductions of about 2 percentage points 1982 on 1975, and middle-income oil importers of about 5 percentage points(1). In theory, one of the 'proper' reactions to external price shocks should have been to adjust investment upwards so as to modify export and import performance to meet the changed structure of world demand, to minimize the impact on the balance of payments, and to substitute other energy resources for oil. In many cases this happened, but, for the poorest countries, raising investment meant either massive injections of foreign capital, or a sacrifice of consumption, or both.

As an illustration, the World Bank (1982) reports that least-developed countries lost 1% of GDP as a result of changes in external prices (including changes in non-energy prices) between 1972 and 1978. That it was not higher is explained by the relatively low ratio of imported oil to GNP in developing countries and by external borrow-

---

*   I would like to express my indebtedness to the Leverhulme Trust for funding the wider programme of work from which this paper is drawn.

ing which enabled a less painful short-run adjustment to energy price rises. This 1% was made up of a reduction in the share of investment in GDP, an increase in foreign borrowing and a rise in the share of consumption, indicating that much borrowing went into consumption or that external finance simply substituted for reduced domestic savings. Only the industrial economies shared this experience of reduced investment shares: all other developing economies and the oil exporters (as one would expect) increased their investment shares. This 'perverse' adjustment in the poorest countries simply reflects the near impossibility of adjusting expectations and plans away from increased consumption, given the already miserably low absolute levels.

With the exception of the poorest countries, however, oil-importing LDCs did react by raising investment ratios. Some managed to expand manufactured exports and, typically, world trade movements favoured this form of adjustment. The exceptions have been in agricultural markets in which protectionism has increased (as in the EEC) and in basic commodity markets where the familiar fluctuations in world prices have worked to the detriment of countries such as Bangladesh, Zambia and Tanzania. But because of the rising cost of imports, the aggregate picture has been one of increasing balance-of-payments deficits, from some $40 billion for all oil-importing LDCs in 1975 to some $82 billion in 1982 (in current prices). Of that $82 billion in 1982, medium- and long-term borrowing financed some $59 billion, of which $40 billion came from private sources. Inevitably, the burden of interest payments has risen and comprised nearly 20% of the value of exports for oil importers in 1982, and a number of countries have been forced into debt renegotiation and rescheduling. Rapid inflation has accompanied the attempts to adjust, with annual rates of price changes in middle-income oil-importing countries standing at over 40% in 1980 and approaching 20% in low-income oil-importing countries.

Overall, then, the story of the 1970s for the oil-importing LDCs has been one of some success in adjusting to rising energy prices and world recession, but with reductions of 1-2% of absolute levels of GDP, rising current-account deficits, debt-servicing problems and rapid inflation. The impact on economic growth has certainly not been as dramatic as many feared, but it is as well to remember that energy price rises were only one of the many factors affecting LDC economic performance in the 1970s. Wallich (1981), for example, draws attention to the fortuitous role of the weather in producing good crops in the South-East Asia region, and the role of workers' remittances in alleviating balance-of-payments problems. Balassa (1981a) notes the completely offsetting effect of increased coffee prices for countries such as Colombia.

But if rising energy prices played their part in depressing the growth prospects of LDCs in the 1970s, will a reversal in energy price trends in the 1980s come as an unmixed blessing?

The impact of lower oil prices
The most obvious and direct impact of lower oil prices will be on the balance of payments via reduced import bills. Net oil importers imported some 5.5 million barrels of oil a day in 1982. If the demand for oil by these countries was completely inelastic, the $5 per barrel reduction in OPEC prices in March 1983 would constitute an outright saving of some $10 billion per year compared to a net trade deficit of some $76 billion. Clearly, these would be substantial gains.

In practice, there will be offsetting factors to such gains. With lower prices, imports will expand. The World Bank (1981) reports a range of energy price elasticities from 0.1 to 0.5 for developing countries. This suggests that the OPEC price fall, if sustained, would tend to increase oil imports to the relevant LDCs by up to 7% or about 150 million barrels a year. At a market price of $29 per barrel this would imply an offsetting $4.35 billion in terms of increased oil imports. The reduction in the import bill due to reduced energy prices could thus be halved compared to the zero elasticity case. Obviously, increased energy imports, properly used, would assist the development effort, especially in those countries where the reaction to increased oil prices has simply been one of outright quantity restriction (see the case study of the Sudan below). Overall, however, we might think of an immediate direct gain to oil-importing LDCs of some $5 billion p.a. on the balance of payments.

One dominant question mark, however, is just how long the 1983 price fall will last. Virtually any guess has its rationale, depending on how one projects the future for the recovery of the world economy, OPEC stability, the impact of energy conservation measures, and so on. One plausible set of projections (UK Department of Energy, 1982) suggests that the price may well fall to $25 a barrel by 1985 but stay constant in real terms thereafter. If so, the benefits to LDCs will be of a once-for-all nature.

The third confounding factor is that the tendency to energy conservation in both developed and developing economies may now be relaxed as energy prices fall. Regardless of the debate about how best to secure energy conservation - by which we mean reductions in the amount of energy used per unit of economic activity - there can be little question that the oil price 'hikes' of 1973 and 1979 have stimulated reductions in energy per unit of GDP over and above the trend for the 'pre-crisis' period. The importance of this is twofold. In the industrialized economies it has helped to keep the demand for oil down and hence to weaken the power, such as it has been, of OPEC to sustain high oil prices by supply restrictions. If the conservation inducement is relaxed as prices fall again, it effectively shifts an element of market power back to OPEC. The other feature is that developing countries have themselves engaged in conservation activity. The experience is widely varied according to the capability of countries to adjust through, for example, technological switches in the industrial use of energy. In some countries, processes have been changed rapidly. In others, the very fact of an exacerbated foreign exchange crisis has meant that already antiquated equipment remains in place. But the World Bank (1981) has suggested that energy-to-GDP ratios in oil-importing countries would have risen to 5.6 barrels of oil equivalent to $1,000 of GDP in 1990 without energy price rises, compared to the then anticipated 4.4 barrels with energy price increases. What matters, then, is whether the fall in prices over the next few years will lead to a relaxation in that expectation of more energy conservation. For some countries, such as South Korea, the answer must be 'no'. For others, it is very likely to be the case.

Other relevant factors will quickly indicate the complexity of gauging the impact of falling oil prices. As we have seen, a number of LDCs 'rode out' the energy price rises of the 1970s because of structural adjustments and/or rises in the world prices of their staple exports. The internal adjustments were encouraged and more than occasionally stimulated by oil price rises. Their success may be sufficient to ensure their continuation and stability. But falling oil prices, and especially falling real oil prices, could easily lead to a relaxation of the resolve to keep on with the adjustment process. As to world markets, these will remain volatile and a $5 fall in the price of oil can quickly be offset by a small fall in the price of basic commodity exports. Thus the index of all primary commodity prices rose in real and money terms to 1977, but in 1981 the real index stood no higher than it was in 1976 and fell in 1981 (IMF, 1982). In effect, the factors that enabled some countries to weather the oil price shocks of the

1970s may be the same ones that eliminate the gains from oil price falls in the 1980s. Possibly offsetting these unknowns will be the extent to which falling oil prices will revive the world economy, lead to an expansion of demand and thus assist LDC exports in terms of both volume and price. Expansionary forces should be at work in oil-dependent industrialized countries such as Japan, while others, such as the United Kingdom, can be net gainers or losers depending on how exchange rates move against the dollar (the price of oil being denominated in dollars).

The effect on OPEC country incomes could be all-important. A 15% price fall, as announced in March 1983, accompanied as it is by quantity restrictions, will reduce OPEC income substantially. Several effects are likely to ensue. In 1981, 0.35% of OECD GNP and 1.5% of OPEC GNP was given as official assistance to LDCs. The OPEC contribution appears all the larger, in terms of ability to lend, given that the percentage from OAPEC GNP was 2.83. While this is a decline from 5% in 1975, the entire reduction is accounted for by the cessation of lending by Iran. Thus, we might now expect a further reduction in the light of oil price reductions, offset to some extent by a political commitment to support Arab LDCs. Another effect will be on the recycling of monetary assets. As OPEC incomes fall, so will the amounts channelled to international banking institutions to lend on.

Among the OPEC countries there are substantial differences. The high-income oil exporters (Kuwait, Libya, Saudi Arabia, Qatar and UAE) will continue to run balance-of-payments surpluses, albeit smaller ones than in the past, and will be able to maintain their level of demand for imports from LDCs. Others, such as Nigeria and Venezuela, are already experiencing difficulties which are rebounding on oil-importing LDCs. For example, Venezuela's decision, with Mexico, to reduce the concessionary loans that they make to offset the cost of their oil exports to nine Central American and Caribbean countries will have adverse economic repercussions. Quantifying all these effects is highly uncertain.

Overall, isolating the impacts of oil price changes is fraught with difficulty. What few generalizations can be made also mask the wide variety of impacts country by country. Some brief case examples will illustrate.

Bangladesh
With a per capita annual income of $130 (1980) Bangladesh provides an example of an economy where the smallest loss

52

of income can have wildly disproportional effects on human welfare. Its GDP growth rate in the 1970s fell to 3.3% p.a. compared to 3.6% p.a. in the 1960s, but the proper comparison for current purposes is between the achieved growth rate and what it would have been without the oil price increases. Wallich (1981b), following the World Bank methodology established by Balassa (1981b), estimates that low-income Asian countries generally (Bangladesh, Burma, India, the Maldives, Nepal, Pakistan and Sri Lanka) gained very slightly, at about 0.2% of 1974-8 GNP, from the rise in export prices relative to the earlier period. They lost some 1.3% of GNP as a result of import price rises. Since world trade contracted, there was also a 'volume effect', and the combined price and volume impacts have been put at 1.95% of GNP.

Bangladesh lost heavily from the movement in the terms of trade (the ratio of export to import prices) which fell by 50% from 1970 to 1978. The extent to which oil price rises can be blamed for such changes is highlighted when one observes that the fall to 1973 was only 13%, with a 40% further drop coming in 1973 on its own and a further 10% drop to 1976. To some extent, the impact was cushioned by the fact that only 25% of Bangladesh's energy consumption is met by commercial sources (Desai, 1981), although this does little to alleviate the impact on such all-important sectors as transport. Moreover, workers' remittances assisted the balance of payments, as did a measure of 'protection' for some exports in that their destination was the Eastern bloc.

With a fall in oil prices, Bangladesh stands to gain directly on the balance of payments. By 1980 oil comprised 10% of the value of all imports to Bangladesh and equalled 25% of the value of exports. The 'diversionary' effect of releasing foreign exchange from payment for oil imports for other uses could thus be very substantial. With a current-account deficit of over $750 million in 1980, such changes are of considerable significance. External debt stands at some $3.5 billion.

But the overriding factor which will influence the energy future of Bangladesh in the 1980s and 1990s is the presence of non-associated gas reserves. In 1980 these were estimated to be equal to 1,680 million barrels of oil equivalent. Recoverable coal reserves are perhaps 500 million tonnes of coal equivalent. Islam (1979) and Desai (1981) indicate that most of the oil used in Bangladesh is consumed by households and the industrial sector. Conversion to gas is possible for the commercial and industrial sector, but more complex for households, although 50% of the Bangladesh population lived in cities of over 500,000 people in 1980 (World Bank, 1982). Arguably, gas in the quantities indicated for Bangladesh could also lead to a developed trade in liquefied natural gas (LNG) in the 1990s. Either way, the potential for displacing oil imports is significant. Bangladesh is thus likely to be a net gainer from the fall in oil prices, assuming that these are not so dramatic as to hinder the prospects for world trade in natural gas. The prospects for jute prices are also encouraging, so that the foundations for a fundamental adjustment to the vagaries of world energy markets exist for Bangladesh.

The Sudan

In 1980 the Sudan had a per capita income of some $410. In terms of energy, something like 85% of all energy consumed comes from 'traditional' sources -wood, charcoal, animal and crop waste (Edwards, Pearce and Sladen, 1983). The story of the 1970s makes dismal reading. High growth rates to 1978 were replaced with negative growth to 1980. Investment has fallen and domestic savings have fallen dramatically. As an almost entirely agricultural nation, the Sudan depends critically upon its exports of cotton and crops of groundnuts, sesame and dura. Yet agricultural productivity has been declining, a function, in the view of most, of the lack of any structured incentive schemes for expanding output or for the optimal choice of crops (Acharya, 1979; Nashashibi, 1981). To date, all liquid fuels have been imported, either as crude oil, which is refined at Port Sudan, or as petroleum products. The complex regional government system of the Sudan means that supplies are carefully allocated to regions independently of the maximum national benefit that might be obtained by a freer distribution system.

The oil price rises of the 1970s effectively paralysed the economy of the Sudan, although, as the general remarks previously make clear, energy alone cannot conceivably be isolated as the cause of economic problems in virtually any developing country in this period. The energy import bill was some $11 million in 1973, and $320 million in 1981. Edwards et al. (1983) estimate that the import bill would have stood at only $34 million in 1981 had the quantity of 1981 imported oil been bought at 1973 prices. Yet this calculation highlights the most important reaction of the Sudan to higher oil prices: despite substantial increases in foreign assistance, the Sudan has simply been unable to secure sufficient foreign exchange to expand its oil imports in physical terms. Thus, 1981 crude oil imports stood at just under 1 million tonnes compared to 850,000 tonnes in 1970. Imports of petroleum products have taken up a little of the excess demand, rising from zero in 1973 to 350 million tonnes in 1981. But the overall effect has been one of constraining and rationing oil demand, with disastrous consequences. In a country heavily dependent on transport and infrastructure, given the vast size of the country and the distances over which produce must travel, especially to Port Sudan for export, the story is one of insufficient fuel supplies, breakdowns, interrupted services and lost output. As noted above, energy prices have been instrumental in these problems, although they by no means account for them. Domestic prices have been allowed to rise in response to external price changes, although the state of excess demand is such that a flourishing black market in oil products survives. In short, what rising oil prices have done to the Sudan is to add one more binding constraint on growth potential.

Ostensibly, then, falling prices should ease that constraint and the most direct impact should be felt via a relaxation of import controls, particularly on petroleum products (crude oil imports are also constrained by the refining capacity at Port Sudan). Whether this will be the reaction is questionable, however, since the Sudan has lived with the import restrictions for a whole decade. Its external debt servicing stands at about 14% of the value of exports, and it is arguable that it will be obliged to take the benefits of oil price falls in the form of honoured debt repayment, especially since it has already negotiated reservicing arrangements with its commercial bank creditors. Either way, falling oil prices would appear as an unmixed blessing for the Sudan, although it may be unable to use that gain to increase domestic consumption or investment in any significant fashion. The outlook is, however, more disturbing when one considers the projection that by 1990 the Sudan could readily find itself in a 'traditional fuel' crisis, i.e. one in which the demand for traditional fuels outstrips the supply. Without foreign exchange constraints, one would expect that excess demand to spill over into oil imports. In the Sudan's case this seems unlikely given the magnitude of the problem.

Perversely, the one bright spot in the Sudan's future may well be injured by the fall in oil prices. Sudan has discovered oil in the Sudd region and drilling is also taking place elsewhere, notably on the Red Sea coast. The nature of the existing finds is uncertain, but a figure of 500,000 tonnes p.a. is quite widely quoted (Edwards et al. 1983). Demand projections suggest that even with these supplies the Sudan will continue to have an energy crisis, but, self-evidently,

55

supplies of this magnitude cannot but benefit its economy. The question mark that surrounds the issue is the cost of production. The oil is located in difficult terrain, and transport and exploration difficulties are commonplace. It seems very unlikely that production would be uneconomical at $25 per barrel. Whether it would continue to attract oil companies at, say, $15 per barrel without a change in production-sharing arrangements is unknown.

This example illustrates one of the apparent paradoxes of the oil price rises of the 1970s. The increases in prices made the development of many sources profitable, and the conspicuous example is the UK North Sea development. How far prices would have to fall to make some of the 1970s developments uneconomic is not generally known, since costs of production are jealously guarded secrets. What must be a possibility, however, is that some marginal sources will cease to be profitable at prices below $20 per barrel. Of wider significance, perhaps, is the fact that it is not only oil and gas exploration that have been stimulated by the oil price rises, but other energy sources which have high extraction costs. The massive expansion in lignite production and exploitation is a case in point.

Brazil

Brazil meets some 75% of its energy demand from commercial energy sources (Eden and Jannuzzi, 1981). Brazil is an oil producer but imports significant quantities of oil as well: about 41 million tonnes in 1977, and by 1979 energy imports to Brazil comprised a staggering 48% of the value of merchandise exports. The effect of oil price increases was a substantial deterioration in the terms of trade in the immediate post-1973 period, but this was offset to some extent by rising coffee and soyabean prices in the next four years. Balassa (1981a) estimates the terms of trade loss for Brazil to have been some 2.2% of GNP for the period 1974-8. Balassa also relates the policy responses which included, as almost universally, increased foreign loans, but also a sustained effort at import substitution. Interestingly, growth rates of the economy increased rather than decreased, thus exacerbating the external deficit as they 'sucked in' imports. In all of this, attempts at substitution policies were directed at pulp and paper, petrochemicals, fertilizers, steel and non-ferrous metals. Balassa estimates that, for 1974-8 as an average, fuels accounted for only 13% of the import substitution gains which ameliorated the balance-of-payments problems. Certainly, Brazil's rate of growth of energy consumption was not markedly less in the second half of the 1970s than it was before the first oil price 'hike'.

How will falling energy prices affect Brazil? Brazil has the capability for expanding coal supplies significantly. Eden and Jannuzzi (1981) suggest that by 2000, coal production could expand from some 2.5 mtoe to 36 mtoe a year. Domestic oil production could be expanded from over 8 mt to 42 mt, gas and liquid propane gas to 11 mtoe, hydropower to 87 mtoe and 'alcohol' (ethanol) to 14 mtoe. All of these increases would be dramatic, but it is significant that Eden and Jannuzzi still forecast imports of oil in the year 2000 of 52 mt. This suggests that Brazil's demand for liquid fuels, almost entirely in the industrial and transport sectors, will outstrip domestic capability, even on favourable assumptions. In that respect, reductions in the price of oil must come as a reasonably unmixed blessing. The offsetting factor is once again the extent to which those price falls make the development of other indigenous energy sources less economic. There must, for example, be serious question marks about alcohol production for 'mixing' with petroleum on precisely these grounds. To pursue these policies suggests that a country like Brazil is placing a very high premium on saving foreign exchange, something that the ratio of debt servicing to merchandise exports suggests is a sound policy. Equally, what has to be borne in mind is the extent to which such a commitment diverts resources away from other export potential, or less costly import-substituting activity. If reductions in the world oil price lead to more careful appraisals of the 'rush' to develop indigenous energy sources (sometimes, it would seem, at almost any cost), it will have an added benefit.

Conclusions
While it is possible to engage in some general analysis of what we might expect by way of benefits to developing countries from reductions in world oil prices, it should be evident that what will actually happen will depend on a host of both interrelated and unrelated factors, and will vary substantially from one country to another. While reduced oil prices must have direct and immediate benefits to the balance of payments of oil importers, the sometimes overlooked benefits of rising prices must not be ignored. In particular, falling prices must not be allowed to slow down the structural adjustments many countries have made and are making, since these can be argued to be appropriate for a world of 'high' or 'comparatively low' oil prices. The incen-

tive to energy conservation should not be reduced either. Finally, there must be no adaptation of policy on the basis that what has happened in 1983 will be sustained for the next two decades. OPEC is not dead, and even if it were, it may well be that it was, in recent years at least, merely acting as a rubber stamp for underlying world market forces. If so, those forces will still be present and could readily lead to a regime of rising world prices in nominal terms, and at least constant real prices, for a long time to come.

Notes

1. Throughout, we use the World Bank's definitions of oil-importing developing countries as all developing countries other than Algeria, Angola, Bahrain, Brunei, Congo, Ecuador, Egypt, Gabon, Indonesia, Iran, Iraq, Malaysia, Mexico, Nigeria, Oman, Peru, Syria, Trinidad and Tobago, Tunisia and Venezuela. 'Low income' countries have per capita incomes below $410 p.a.

References

S.N. Acharya (1979), Incentives for Resource Allocation: A Case Study of Sudan, World Bank Staff Working Paper No. 367, December 1979 (Washington, DC, World Bank).

B. Balassa(1981a), 'Policy Responses to External Shocks in Selected Latin American Countries', Quarterly Review of Economics and Business, No.2, Summer 1981, pp.131-64.

B. Balassa(1981b), Adjustments to External Shocks in Developing Economies, World Bank Staff Working Paper No. 472, August 1981 (Washington, DC, World Bank).

A. Desai (1981), 'Effects of the Rise in Oil Prices on South Asian Countries 1972-1978', International Labour Review, Vol. 120, No.2, March-April, pp.129-47.

R. Eden and G. Jannuzzi (1981), Brazil: the Energy Outlook, Energy Research Group, Cavendish Laboratory, University of Cambridge, Energy Discussion Paper 10.

R. Edwards, D.W. Pearce and J. Sladen (1983), The Effect of Oil Price Increases on the Economy of Sudan (Geneva, International Labour Office, draft).

IMF (1982), World Economic Outlook, Occasional Paper 9 (Washington, DC, IMF).

R. Islam (1979), Some Economic Implications of Higher Oil Prices: the Case of Bangladesh, International Labour Office, World Employment Programme Working Paper (Geneva, ILO).

K. Nashashibi (1981), 'A Supply Framework for Exchange Reform in Developing Countries: the Experience of the Sudan', IMF Staff Papers.

P. Nunnenkamp (1982), 'The Impact of Rising Oil Prices on Economic Growth in Developing Countries in the Seventies', Kyklos, Fasc. 4, Vol. 35, 1982, pp.633-47.

J. Powelson (1977), 'The Oil Price Increase: Impacts on Industrialised and less Developed Countries', Journal of Energy and Development, Vol. 3, No.1, pp.10-25.

UK Government (1982), Oil Prices in the Long Term (London, UK Department of Energy).

C. Wallich (1981), An Analysis of Developing Country Adjustment Experiences in the 1970s: Low Income Asia, World Bank Staff Working Paper No. 487, August 1981 (Washington, DC, World Bank).

World Bank (1981), World Development Report 1981 (London, Oxford University Press).

World Bank (1982), World Development Report 1982 (London, Oxford University Press).

4 The USSR and Eastern Europe

Jonathan P. Stern

At the foot of tables showing world energy statistics, one often finds a note to the effect that the figures exclude centrally planned economies. This has become such standard practice that readers rarely question whether, if these countries were included, the picture would be radically different. This chapter will be devoted largely to the USSR but will also include some reflections on the six East European countries of the Council for Mutual Economic Assistance (CMEA)*. It will be concerned not simply with the impact that lower oil prices might have in these countries, but with the role that the region, and particularly the USSR, may play in international energy trade and pricing, with reference mainly to oil, but also to natural gas.

The USSR is by far the largest oil producer in the world, reaching the annual figure of 614 million tonnes (mt) in 1982; and in 1983, at a planned 529 billion cubic metres (bcm), it may surpass the United States to become the world's largest producer of natural gas as well. It is also a world leader in the production of coal and has a significant development of hydroelectric and nuclear power. It currently exports some 70 mt of oil and 32 of gas per year to its East European allies(1). In the case of some countries (such as Bulgaria and Czechoslovakia), nearly the totality of their imports of liquid and gaseous fuels come from the USSR. The rise in oil prices during 1979-80 forced them back increasingly upon Soviet supplies and greatly complicated their economies, despite the fact that fuel imports from the USSR are traded largely on soft currency terms. Romania was a net oil exporter until the mid-1970s, when falling production and rising domestic consumption led to a situation where, by

---

* Bulgaria, Czechoslovakia, the German Democratic Republic, Hungary, Poland and Romania.

1980, the country was importing half of its requirements from the Middle East. Despite repeated requests, Romania has failed to obtain oil from the USSR on concessionary terms (the country does import very small quantities from the Soviet Union but on hard currency terms and at world market prices), but has had more success with natural gas, where it imports 1.5 bcm per year - a much smaller quantity than other countries but on the same soft currency terms. Soviet deliveries of oil and oil products to other CMEA countries (including the non-European members: Cuba, Mongolia and Vietnam) were planned to be 80 mt per year in the 1981-5 period. In the event, the deliveries to certain East European countries have been cut, in some cases up to 10% starting in 1982; natural gas deliveries appear to have been held at around 32 bcm per year. East European imports of oil from the world market were probably around 15 mt in 1982; when one subtracts from this figure 10.9 mt for Romania and 1 mt imported by the GDR under its special relationship with the Federal Republic, this means that the other four countries have been forced virtually to eliminate their world market oil trade and to depend to an even greater extent on Soviet deliveries within the framework of CMEA integration and cooperation(2).

The impact of lower world oil prices on the USSR
Rapidly increasing Soviet oil production in the 1960s and 1970s allowed the Soviets to expand deliveries to Eastern Europe and also to the world market. Throughout the 1970s the level of Soviet oil exports to the hard currency area remained in the 35-50 mt range, but, as Table 2 shows, the importance to the Soviet economy of this trade greatly increased. The value of Soviet oil exports to the hard currency area rose from $0.6 bn in 1971 to $11.2 bn in 1981(3); more significantly, this represented 22% of total Soviet hard currency earnings at the beginning of the decade, but a staggering 58% at the later date. Thus, with the continuing low quality of Soviet manufactured goods and the absence of any other commodities readily saleable on Western markets (except raw materials such as gold and diamonds), energy, and particularly oil, had become an irreplaceable item in the Soviet hard currency trade balance.

This is not the place to explain in any detail the importance of hard currency earnings to the Soviet economy. The agricultural problems of the Soviet Union have received considerable coverage, and there is little reason to suppose that the country will not continue to experience years when

Table 4.1   Soviet energy production: planned (p) and actual (a)

(Oil and coal in million tonnes, gas in billion cubic metres, electric power in billion kilowatt hours.)

	Oil (p)	Oil (a)	Natural gas (p)	Natural gas (a)	Coal (p)	Coal (a)	Electric power (p)	Electric power (a)
1971	371.3	371.8	211	211.0	620.4	640.9	790	800.4
1975	496.0	490.8	300-320	289.3	690.0	701.3	1050	1039.0
1976	520.0	517.9	313	321.0	715.0	711.5	1095	1111.0
1977	550.0	545.8	342	346.0	733.0	722.1	1160	1150.0
1978	575.0	571.5	370	372.2	750.0	723.6	1225	1202.0
1979	593.0	585.6	401	407.6	775.0	718.7	1300	1239.0
1980	640.0	603.2	435	435.2	805.0	716.4	1380	1295.0
1981	610.0	609.0	458	465.0	738.0	704.0	1335	1325.0
1982	614.0	613.0	492	501.0	-	718.0	-	1366.0
1983	619.0	-	529	-	723.0	-	1405	-
1985	630.0	-	630	-	775.0	-	1555	-

Table 4.2   Soviet hard currency earning from energy exports in value (current dollar millions) and as a percentage of total hard currency earnings

	Oil and oil products Value	Oil and oil products %	Natural gas Value	Natural gas %	Coal and coke Value	Coal and coke %	Total Energy %
1971	567	21.6	20	0.7	124	4.7	27.0
1972	556	19.9	23	0.8	230	8.2	28.9
1973	1,248	26.1	23	0.5	134	2.8	29.4
1974	2,548	34.1	86	1.2	251	3.4	38.7
1975	3,176	40.5	209	2.7	390	5.0	48.2
1976	4,514	46.4	347	3.6	368	3.8	53.8
1977	5,275	46.5	566	5.0	357	3.1	54.6
1978	5,716	43.4	1,063	8.1	293	2.2	53.7
1979	8,932	45.7	1,431	7.3	314	1.6	54.6
1980	10,803	46.7	2,558	11.1	340	1.5	59.3
1981	11,222	58.3	3,999	20.8	177	0.9	80.0

Source: Figures to 1979 are from Paul G. Ericson and Ronald S. Millar, 'Soviet Foreign Economic Behaviour: A Balance of Payments Perspective', in Soviet Economy in a Time of Change, Joint Economic Committee, US Congress, 10 October 1979, Volume 2, Appendix H, p. 242. Later figures are author's estimates and may therefore not be strictly comparable with earlier figures.

grain purchases are particularly important (albeit, perhaps, not with such regularity as in the past five years). The question of imports of high technology goods and equipment is one on which opinion is more divided, but there is a consensus that it is important for the USSR to continue to have access to these commodities, and there are many who would regard this as indispensable to a resumption of appreciable Soviet economic growth. In the period 1981-2, these two factors were compounded by a need felt by Moscow to step in and prevent Poland defaulting on its hard currency credit obligations to Western countries. The debt problems of Eastern Europe were causing Western commercial banks to squeeze the USSR on its short-term debt obligations, and this led to an unprecedented need for hard currency in Moscow. The combination of these events resulted in record sales of oil and oil products on Western markets, sometimes at considerable discounts.

Since 1976 we have unfortunately been denied Soviet official statistics of oil and product exports in volume terms, but according to OECD estimates, net Soviet crude oil and product exports to the OECD area fell from 56.6 mt in 1980 to 51.6 mt in 1981(4). However, preliminary indications for 1982 suggest that this figure rose sharply, perhaps to as much as 65 mt. In the first three months of 1983, Soviet oil exports appeared to rise still further, to perhaps as much as 1.6 million barrels per day (equivalent to some 80 mt on a yearly basis), but there would appear to be some amounts of Libyan oil exported on behalf of the Soviet Union included in this figure. The reason for the jump was clearly the need for increased revenues already mentioned, combined with the fact that a slack world oil market and the fall in oil prices make it very difficult for the USSR to raise such revenues. During the 1970s, Soviet oil trade with the West tended to be on yearly contracts. In the most recent period, the USSR has been forced to sell smaller cargoes wherever it could find a market, sometimes being compelled to take very significant discounts on shipments. This situation was in marked contrast to Soviet experience in the 1970s when two sharp oil price increases produced substantial and unexpected windfalls of hard currency which were welcome in a time of expanding trade with the West. The fall in the price of oil was particularly unwelcome for the USSR in that it arrived at a time of unprecedented need for hard currency.

It is quite remarkable that the USSR has been able to expand its oil exports to the extent that occurred in 1982. In the 1970s most commentators (even while not agreeing with the CIA 1977 analysis that the CMEA contries would be importing $3\frac{1}{2}$ to $4\frac{1}{2}$ million b/d of oil by 1985) were predicting that by the mid-1980s Soviet oil exports to the West could have dwindled to near zero. The fact that this has not happened is significant, particularly given the sharp reduction in the rate of increase in Soviet oil production (to just 1% in 1982). This means not only that the USSR has cut back considerably on its domestic consumption of oil as well as on deliveries to Eastern Europe, but that unless further draconian measures are taken to curtail domestic consumption, Soviet exports to the West have reached a physical maximum. They almost certainly cannot be maintained at 65 mt annually, let alone the much higher levels of 1983, unless Soviet oil conservation and substitution are much more successful in the short term than is anticipated and/or Soviet economic growth rates, and hence domestic oil consumption, remain extremely low. This is a short-term judgment for the next five years. After that time, it is conceivable either that Soviet oil production increases will speed up again or that conservation measures in respect of oil will have begun to bite. The former is unlikely because Soviet energy investment priorities have changed, as will be shown below.

The Soviets therefore face a short-term problem: that, at current levels of exports, a fall in the oil price of one dollar reduces their earnings by around \$450m per year. Moreover, a look at the CMEA oil balance suggests that it will not be possible to raise volume sales any further, and that it will probably be necessary to reduce them. The question of how big a problem this will be relates to the Soviet Union's short-term hard currency requirements. It has always been an open question how, and in what time-frame, the USSR calculates its hard currency requirements. I have always leaned towards a perception of a guaranteed 'baseload' hard currency earning capacity, which can be topped up with commodities such as gold as and when the need arises. It is interesting that when the need did arise, the authorities decided to sell oil rather than other commodities such as gold. Part of the explanation may be that it is the planners who make the decisions on oil sales and who can require the Ministry to make sales, despite a falling market; whereas, in the case of gold, it is the bankers who take the merchandising decisions and would have strongly resisted raising sales on a falling market. It would appear that, in the period since early 1982, the requirement to earn revenues has been so strong that the planners have instructed the relevant ministries to sell the maximum possible quantities on world markets. It is extremely difficult to forecast whether requirements of convertible currency for imports and the Soviet liquidity position during the near future will continue to force them to maintain this policy, and therefore how easily the USSR would be able to survive a short period of falling world oil prices. But a world oil price trend which showed real declines over a period of, for example, five years would cause the USSR considerable inconvenience because it is very unlikely that a year of large grain imports could be avoided over this time-frame (indeed there is a view that even with good harvests the country will require continued substantial purchases of grains), and this would mean ensuring that sufficient convertible currency earning potential were available to cover such an eventuality.

In 1982-3 the Soviets have been unfortunate in that their needs were urgent. As a result, in some cases they have been obliged to give substantial discounts on their oil sales, thus recalling the 1960s when they gained a reputation for being prepared to undersell the market to a very large extent in order to raise revenues. This reputation lasted a great deal longer than the actual practice. Once the USSR came to be an accepted actor in world oil trade, the country followed the market very closely; it is a very recent phenomenon which once again sees them discounting foreign oil sales. However, in April 1983, with the Soviets selling as much as 1.5 to 1.6 million b/d on world oil markets, OPEC was forced to approach the USSR about its oil price behaviour. The perception was that Soviet cooperation might have become essential to market stability, since the USSR was one of the first of the major oil exporters officially to lower its selling prices, making two cuts in February and March of 1983 which brought Urals crude down to $27.50. The approach may have had some effect, since at the end of April Soviet crude prices were raised to $28.50, but it is more likely that Soyuznefte-export had simply been instructed to raise the price when it was judged that the market had firmed up.

Moscow has consistently refused to be bound by any rules of pricing in its marketing of fuels. In 1973-4 it was accused by some OPEC contries of making huge profits by selling oil to embargoed importing countries at vastly inflated prices. Before 1983 OPEC had never attempted to include the USSR in any kind of pricing agreement and Moscow has never shown any signs of being interested in such an arrangement. The hallmark of the Soviets' oil price policy will continue to be flexibility.

The USSR could be a significant destabilizing force in world oil markets if it should decide to offer substantial discounts from agreed OPEC and North Sea price levels. However, its experience in the oil market should mean that it will avoid starting a price collapse by accident - it is difficult to see any advantage for Moscow in deliberately precipitating instability in the market - but if the situation should remain fragile and Soviet revenue needs should become more acute, one could not rule out the possibility.

The two caveats which have been introduced above with respect to Soviet oil availability, requirements and behaviour have been those of timing and investment priority. What has happened in the Soviet energy balance since the Second World War is that it moved from what one might term the 'coal era' to the 'oil era' and is now entering the 'gas era'. As Soviet oil (and coal) production has slowed down, gas production has speeded up, and the plans for the expansion of the pipeline network from Siberia to the west of the country (six trunk pipelines, each carrying some 35 bcm of gas - 30 mtoe - of which only one will be the export pipeline to Western Europe) suggest that investment priorities have been shifted to reflect this new strategy. What this means for Soviet fuel export strategy (to both the hard-currency and the non-hard-currency area) is that it becomes far more attractive to export natural gas and retain increasingly scarce oil for domestic consumption. Natural gas has another advantage over oil as an export commodity to the hard-currency area: it is sold on long-term - 20 to 25-year - contracts, and hence the income is much more predictable for a planned economy, which has a great need for long-term dependable earnings. It is for this reason that some of the new Soviet gas contracts include a minimum price for the first year of deliveries. However, natural gas will not provide an immediate panacea for Soviet hard currency earnings, the disadvantage of this kind of fuel export being its inflexibility. The USSR has been able to make some 'spot' gas sales to West European countries over the past year, due to spare capacity in the pipeline network, but it is unlikely that these sales are very large.

Table 2 shows that natural gas has greatly increased its share of foreign exchange earnings, to some 20% of the total. In the future, the share of this fuel can be expected to rise greatly, but it is important to recognize that there is a considerable time-lag between the commencement of gas flows and a hard currency surplus. This lag occurs because of the 'package' concept of Soviet gas export projects, by which the imports of equipment from Western countries are, in the first stages of the contract, paid for from the revenues earned from gas exports. It can be estimated that, because

Table 4.1   Soviet energy production: planned (p) and actual (a)

(Oil and coal in million tonnes, gas in billion cubic metres, electric power in billion kilowatt hours.)

	Oil (p)	Oil (a)	Natural gas (p)	Natural gas (a)	Coal (p)	Coal (a)	Electric power (p)	Electric power (a)
1971	371.3	371.8	211	211.0	620.4	640.9	790	800.4
1975	496.0	490.8	300-320	289.3	690.0	701.3	1050	1039.0
1976	520.0	517.9	313	321.0	715.0	711.5	1095	1111.0
1977	550.0	545.8	342	346.0	733.0	722.1	1160	1150.0
1978	575.0	571.5	370	372.2	750.0	723.6	1225	1202.0
1979	593.0	585.6	401	407.6	775.0	718.7	1300	1239.0
1980	640.0	603.2	435	435.2	805.0	716.4	1380	1295.0
1981	610.0	609.0	458	465.0	738.0	704.0	1335	1325.0
1982	614.0	613.0	492	501.0	-	718.0	-	1366.0
1983	619.0	-	529	-	723.0	-	1405	-
1985	630.0	-	630	-	775.0	-	1555	-

Table 4.2   Soviet hard currency earning from energy exports in value (current dollar millions) and as a percentage of total hard currency earnings

	Oil and oil products Value	Oil and oil products %	Natural gas Value	Natural gas %	Coal and coke Value	Coal and coke %	Total Energy %
1971	567	21.6	20	0.7	124	4.7	27.0
1972	556	19.9	23	0.8	230	8.2	28.9
1973	1,248	26.1	23	0.5	134	2.8	29.4
1974	2,548	34.1	86	1.2	251	3.4	38.7
1975	3,176	40.5	209	2.7	390	5.0	48.2
1976	4,514	46.4	347	3.6	368	3.8	53.8
1977	5,275	46.5	566	5.0	357	3.1	54.6
1978	5,716	43.4	1,063	8.1	293	2.2	53.7
1979	8,932	45.7	1,431	7.3	314	1.6	54.6
1980	10,803	46.7	2,558	11.1	340	1.5	59.3
1981	11,222	58.3	3,999	20.8	177	0.9	80.0

Source: Figures to 1979 are from Paul G. Ericson and Ronald S. Millar, 'Soviet Foreign Economic Behaviour: A Balance of Payments Perspective', in Soviet Economy in a Time of Change, Joint Economic Committee, US Congress, 10 October 1979, Volume 2, Appendix H, p. 242. Later figures are author's estimates and may therefore not be strictly comparable with earlier figures.

of low prices in Soviet gas contracts, gas exports in the 1970s earned virtually no surplus over the debt obligations incurred by the equipment imports until 1980.

The same situation will pertain to the new Soviet gas export contracts, particularly since the volumes currently contracted - 21 bcm as against an originally proposed 40 bcm - are much smaller than originally envisaged (although they may be boosted at a later stage by 8 bcm for Italy and smaller quantities from other countries; see Table 3). Deliveries are scheduled to begin at the end of 1984 and will build to final contract volume around 1987-8, given that there is some flexibility in contract terms such that importing countries are not obliged to take the full contract volume each year.

Although one has to make some assumptions about the price of gas, the cost of the equipment to the USSR and the interest rates on credit (none of these details has been published, and in any case it would require some prediction about how the gas prices would move over the next three years), it appears likely that, if the contracted level remains at 21 bcm, the USSR will require some 4-5 years to pay off the debts it has incurred: i.e. that the new gas contracts will not begin earning a hard currency surplus until around 1989-90. (It could be sooner if additional supplies of gas are commissioned by West European countries.)

This analysis leads to two conclusions. First, natural gas cannot earn significantly greater volumes of hard currency in the short to medium term and probably not until after 1990; hence whatever problem the USSR may be facing with respect to falling oil prices, natural gas exports cannot fully make up the loss in convertible currency earnings. Second, for the USSR the price of internationally traded gas, its relationship with the price of oil, the dimensions of the future gas market in Western Europe and the competition that it may face in that market will become very important issues in the future.

The impact in Eastern Europe
As for the effect that falling oil prices will have on the East European countries, the signs are very contradictory. The most immediate observation, given what has been said above, is that to the extent that the Soviet hard currency crunch requires it to export more oil to the West, there is likely to be even less for these countries on concessionary terms. The Soviets have already made it quite clear that (at least through the 1980s) there will be no increments of oil deliv-

eries to Eastern Europe and there may even be reductions. Having said this, it makes sense to consider Romania separately from the other five East European CMEA members.

For Romania, the effect of lower oil prices will almost certainly be positive, but it is difficult to put a figure on the potential advantage. This is because, although the country imported some 10.9 mt of oil from the world market in 1982, it is uncertain whether imports will continue at these levels while the products which it processes from these imports continue to face depressed world markets and prices. Reports from Romania suggest a dramatic cut in imports of crude oil from the world market in 1983 and a commensurate drop in exports of oil products for hard currency. The large investment in refining capacity made at the end of the 1970s, in order to give the country hard currency earning capacity as a transit refiner, has so far proved to be a disastrous mistake. It may be that the country sustains a smaller loss by keeping refinery capacity as much as 50% underutilized, than by importing crude oil at world market prices to process products which it is unable to resell at a profit. However, when world oil product demand and prices begin to pick up, the country's position will improve.

For the other five countries, the near-term situation will continue to be very difficult even if oil prices fall considerably. With their lack of hard currency and current debt levels, their best hope must be that if prices fall, the repercussions in the producing countries will be such as to make barter trade in soft currencies more attractive. However, it is difficult to see a great deal of complementarity between OPEC and Eastern Europe. In too many cases in the past, the oil producers have found that CMEA goods are less satisfactory and of less high quality than Western counterparts. The hope in Eastern Europe must be that a country which has been greatly alienated from the West, and which has a large consumption requirement, may be willing to enter into soft currency transactions, bartering oil for goods and services. Iran would be the most obvious candidate for such a trade, but at mid-1983, the Islamic Republic appeared to be becoming increasingly hostile to the USSR. It remains to be seen whether this will spill over to include the East European countries. However, if the East Europeans were to open themselves up to the instabilities of trading on the world market, they would be more subject to disruptions as a result of a political change in the oil-exporting countries.

The small volumes of refined product exports which

earned East European countries (other than Romania) some very useful hard currency have been curtailed over the past year, although the GDR and Bulgaria are still able to supplement their earnings in this way. A most positive sign for the region has been the recovery of Polish coal production within a far shorter time than many thought possible. In 1982, production amounted to 189.3 mt, with exports of 28.5 mt, both of which come close to the levels achieved in 1980. The country also began to win back its export markets in the West, with 15.6 mt being delivered to customers in 1982 (although not all of this volume earned hard currency).

In their transactions with the USSR it can be seen that oil will become much more expensive on soft currency terms. Table 4 shows a scenario which is based on reports from East European countries on the price they are paying for oil from the USSR and the way in which this has changed over time. This table contains many different assumptions and differs from the 'Bucharest formula', by which the current year's price is stated to be a rolling average of the previous five years. In the table, the price for the current year is calculated by taking the average of the price on 1 January of the previous four years plus the price on 1 January of the current year(5). In this scenario it appears that if the price of oil falls even slightly, then by 1984 the East European countries will be paying in excess of the world price of oil in soft currency terms by a margin of around 10%. This would be the first time since 1973 that the price that the East European countries pay for Soviet oil has equalled or surpassed that of the world price, and would be an event of immense political significance for intra-bloc relations. However, it must be remembered, first, that this price is paid in soft currency terms and therefore it is erroneous to imagine that Eastern Europe could buy the oil more cheaply elsewhere. Second, it is important to remember that oil is just one commodity, albeit an extremely important one, in the complex structure of CMEA economic integration; although it may also be important in terms of the political and strategic relationship. For East European countries as a whole, therefore, a fall in the price of oil will not necessarily make a big impact on their very difficult energy situation. Their main tasks will still be to practise as much conservation as is possible within the shortest possible time and to substitute anything that can be domestically produced for increasingly scarce oil.

Notes

1. The oil figure is misleading in this context. It represents my calculation of the current level of Soviet exports to Eastern Europe on soft currency terms. The countries can, and do, purchase additional quantities on hard currency terms.
2. The energy relationship between Eastern Europe and the USSR is dealt with in some detail in Jonathan P. Stern, East European Energy and East-West Trade in Energy, British Institutes' Joint Energy Policy Programme, Energy Paper No. 1 (London, Policy Studies Institute/Chatham House, 1982).
3. A number of sources give a substantially higher figure - up to $12.5 bn - for hard currency oil exports in 1981. The difference arises principally from my more restricted definition of the countries which pay in dollars for Soviet oil and the fact that I do not include re-exported Libyan and Iraqi crude in calculations of Soviet hard currency earnings.
4. OECD/IEA, Quarterly Oil Statistics, Third Quarter 1982, pp.128-9.
5. The reason for changing the basis of the calculations is that only in this way can one begin to make the figures square with such scantily published data as we have for intra-bloc prices. For example, in April and June 1981 Poland and Hungary were reported to be paying 92 and 93 rubles per tonne respectively for soviet oil (Energy in Countries with Planned Economies, No. 6, June 1981, p.13). In January 1983, the Polish Foreign Trade Minister stated that Poland would be paying 138.9 rubles per tonne for Soviet oil in 1983 compared with 116.5 rubles per tonne in 1982 (Financial Times, 19 January 1983). Of course, to cite one East European price for Soviet oil is simply a convenient generalization. An excellent West German analysis, also concerned with the impact of falling oil prices on CMEA countries, contains a breakdown of prices for Soviet oil on a country-by-country basis. Jochen Bethkenhagen, Die Auswirkungen der Olpreissenkungen auf die USSR and die ubrigen RGW-Lander, Aktuelle Analysen No. 9 (Cologne, Bundesinstitut fur Ostwissenschaftliche und Internationale Studien, 1983). In addition, there is a very detailed analysis by Professor Marie Lavigne ('The Soviet Union Inside Comecon', Soviet Studies, Vol. 35, No.2, 1983, pp.135-53) in which she recalculates Soviet oil prices within CMEA. Using her figures, my formula works out almost exactly to the 'effective price' she quotes in Table 1.

5 The International Financial System

Kenneth King*

Oil represents 5% of world income at its present price of $29 a barrel. Cheaper oil will not only affect trade balances; it will also affect international capital flows. Depending on whether they are already in balance-of-payments deficit or surplus, oil importers will have smaller borrowing require-ments or larger sums to invest, and oil exporters will have larger borrowing requirements or smaller sums to invest. Shifts in a country's trade and financial flows will affect its exchange rate.

In the financial sector the size of any fall in the price of oil will be less important than the speed with which it occurs. A gradual decline to a lower price would alter some aspects of the international financial system but would leave its framework intact. A sudden drop in the oil price would be sufficient to induce the threatening financial crisis, with adverse repercussions which would for the time being out-weigh the advantages of a lower price.

The effects of a decline in oil prices

A change in the impact of the OPEC producers on the international capital market took place in 1982 when, for the first time since the oil price increase of 1973, OPEC had a net deficit on current account. This was caused much more by a reduction in the volume exported than by the weakness of the oil price. The OPEC current account deficit in 1984, assuming, say, a $20 oil price, would be $100 billion, provided OPEC managed to maintain present export volumes and achieve some limited cuts in imports. The effect of this on Eurodollar markets is not necessarily a contractionary one, since an OPEC deficit must be reflected in a corres-

---

*   This chapter is based on an earlier paper which I wrote with my colleague Kate Mortimer.

ponding surplus (or reduction in deficits) elsewhere. What would be likely to change is the way in which the funds were deployed. The major OPEC exporters initially placed their funds in short-term dollar instruments but then diversified into a wide range of financial and physical assets. The new beneficiaries of the OPEC deficit would have a different attitude to the deployment of their funds. Countries like Japan, already in current account surplus, would have much larger surpluses. They might hav e different investment priorities. Differences in investor preference are fairly readily taken into account by international capital markets; there may be some changes in the relative prices and yields of financial assets, but the most significant feature of such a move is likely to be that the holder of financial securities will be, say, Japanese instead of Arab.

Countries like Brazil and India which experienced improvements in their current account positions would react by expanding domestic activity and drawing in further imports. In these circumstances, world economic activity might rise as financial resources were transferred from countries which did not have a balance-of-payments constraint to countries which did. This could cause some contraction in the supply of funds to Euromarkets, which might lead to upward pressure on interest rates. Countries with improved current account positions would, however, be reducing their demands for funds, and the net impact on interest rates would be small.

Oil transactions have been carried out in US dollars for many years. A low oil price would reduce the demand for dollars in international transactions. The funds thus freed would be available to finance other sorts of activity and could exert some downward pressure on interest rates. More significantly, this source of demand for dollars would be reduced and new holders of these balances might wish to hold other currencies instead of dollars. This could generate a source of dollar weakness that would last for some months.

Much of the immediate impact of cheap oil on foreign exchange markets would come through the effects on capital market flows, but the direct impact on countries' balance-of-payments prospects would be at least as important. This would be dramatic for many countries. Japan, for example, has oil imports which at current prices form half of its total imports of goods. The Japanese yen could be expected to strengthen sharply against almost all other currencies. The strength of the yen would have a large effect on the competitive position of Japanese industry during the 1980s and might well lessen the need for the sort of protectionist measures now being developed by the European Community and the United States. Other countries are also large net importers of oil.

At the other extreme, many oil-exporting countries earn the major part of their export income from oil: Venezuela (95%), Mexico (70%) and the Gulf States are the most dramatic examples of this group. There are other countries where the impact of cheap oil would be important but not overwhelming: for example, the United States, according to most commentators, is expected to have a current account deficit of $30 billion in 1983, but this would be transformed into balance or a surplus by an oil price of twenty dollars a barrel. Similarly, the United Kingdom, currently expecting a £2-3 billion surplus on current account in 1983, would find this reduced to balance or a deficit. The impact of this scale of move is of limited significance. British net exports of oil are 8% of export earnings, and a 30% fall in the price of oil would thus result in a 2.5% fall in export earnings. A deterioration of this size could be wiped out by more rapid growth in British export markets so that the impact of even a sharp fall in the price of oil on the exchange rate might be limited once its initial adverse impact on confidence in sterling had been overcome.

The impact of the oil price on the currencies of some oil exporters could be expected to be very great indeed. But exports of oil will be almost completely insensitive to movements in exchange rates such as the Saudi rial and the Venezuelan bolivar. These exchange rates would be devalued (as the bolivar has been already) to constrain imports rather than to generate larger oil exports. Movements in such exchange rates should be limited because they will have little effect on the countries' trade balances.

Any decline in the price of oil will worsen the debt problem of those oil-exporting countries whose import needs exceed export revenues: Algeria, Angola, Ecuador, Egypt, Indonesia, Malaysia, Mexico, Nigeria and Venezuela. Most of these have, until now, been able to borrow readily because the banks believed export earnings from oil justified lending to them. Mexico and Nigeria have already had to reschedule their debt, and Mexico has said that any reduction in the market price of Saudi oil from its present level of $29 would oblige it to reopen debt negotiations. Not all of the others would be obliged to reschedule their debt even in the event of twenty-dollar oil, but the heavier borrowers would.

There may be a compensating factor to this: oil-importing countries would find their import bill reduced. Brazil

74

would be the most noteworthy beneficiary in terms of the countries currently engaged in debt rescheduling: its current account would improve by about six billion dollars if a twenty-dollar price were to prevail for the next year. This improvement, in conjunction with the measures taken to improve Brazil's external trade position, would offer the banks some reason to view their Brazilian loans more favourably. South Korea would also benefit greatly.

It is almost impossible properly to assess how the credit standing of the major banks would be affected by further rescheduling. On the one hand, the regulatory authorities are encouraging the banks to continue to extend credit to poor credit risks and, by implication, endorsing their existing debt exposures. On the other hand, it is obvious that this sovereign debt exposure to countries which have already rescheduled their debt once is causing a deterioration in the balance sheets of the banks concerned. After all, the cash-flow consequences of rescheduling debt, especially short-term debt, are adverse. They are doubly so when the banks involved are obliged to lend new funds to the country concerned so that it can 'pay' interest on the debt on which it is effectively in default.

The first round of the crisis
A sudden, large fall in the price of oil would cause dramatic changes in international financial flows to which the international financial system would have difficulty in adjusting. Changes of similar magnitude occurred - though in a different direction - during the two periods of rapid oil price increases in the 1970s and the financial system responded rapidly. It might be able to adapt flexibly to the new environment associated with a suddenly low oil price. But international financial institutions have recently been seriously weakened. A sudden fall in the price of oil would weaken them further. It would convert a near-crisis to a full-blown one. This crisis would have consequences extending far beyond the problems banks would face. It would set in motion contractionary forces that would more than offset any favourable impact on world activity of the fall in the price of oil for a period of a year or more.

The international financial system has already been through the first round of a crisis. More than twenty-five sovereign borrowers (that is, national governments) have rescheduled their external bank debt. The amount of this debt far exceeds the net worth of the banks that lent them the funds. If these banks were obliged to classify the rescheduled debt as irrecoverable, then many of them, perhaps most of them, would have a negative net worth - they would be technically bankrupt. At present they can claim that the debt will be repaid and that interest payments on the debt are being made; therefore the problem of 'bad debts' does not arise. The banks concerned are not just small or reckless institutions; almost every major bank's credit standing would be called into question by a series of defaults by sovereign borrowers.

The likelihood of a default or series of defaults has increased. The borrowers are well aware that the banks need them much more than they now need the banks. Mexico has successfully insisted that it would accept a rescheduling agreement only when the banks which had lent it funds agreed to lend it further money (effectively to finance interest payments on existing debt). This means that the banks find their lending to Mexico growing, not falling. Brazil imposed its own rescheduling conditions almost on a 'take it or leave it' basis. Other countries have been somewhat less exigent, but the final effect of their demands is little different. The banks have large amounts of low-quality assets which reduce their credit standing in financial markets.

There is a new approach to rescheduling. The defaulting country demands that its creditors roll over all existing debt for an indeterminate period regardless of the maturity or form of the original credit. This has an initial favourable effect on the capital account of the country concerned: there are no net outflows because banks are obliged to maintain short-term lending, interbank lines and trade credit. The wider repercussions of such an approach are damaging. The banking committee of any lending institution used to take into consideration the maturity structure of different debt instruments and the extent to which certain kinds of borrowing were self-liquidating. Given the precedent set by Mexico, banks can no longer distinguish between, say, a one-week interbank line and a ten-year credit: the risk on both is identical if the country concerned demands the rescheduling of all debt. Trade credit, traditionally the safest form of foreign lending, is now being treated as quasi-sovereign debt by some authorities - they do not provide foreign exchange to permit importers to settle obligations.

The causes of the current wave of rescheduling are beyond the scope of this chapter. A large amount of the borrowing was undertaken to finance balance-of-payments deficits that were a response to sudden sharp increases in oil

76

import bills - but this does not explain the debt problems of less developed countries that are oil exporters. There was a large amount of imprudent borrowing in the inflationary 1970s. The other side of this is that there was a large amount of imprudent lending by banks to countries with no prospect of servicing that debt. In the 1980s the borrowers are no longer able to carry on borrowing to fund liabilities incurred earlier - let alone to fund continuing current account deficits. It is widely thought that banks should be made to face the consequences of their lending policies in the 1970s - and this explains the political pressures that make monetary authorities in the USA and Europe reluctant to provide assistance to their banks.

The first round of the international financial crisis in 1982 was resolved by a series of short-term measures involving operations by the Federal Reserve Bank, the Bank for International Settlements and the International Monetary Fund. Loans to the central banks of countries that were otherwise going to be obliged to default were made on the basis of a series of bilateral negotiations. These short-term measures were supplemented by a longer-term one: the agreement to increase IMF quotas by 50%. It is open to question how much this agreement was the result of the financial crisis - some increase in quotas would have taken place anyway - but certainly in the case of the USA the crisis did cause a more ready acceptance of the need for increased quotas. The increase in quotas already seems small in relation to the size of the debt problems of the countries engaged in rescheduling their international bank borrowings.

With the ending of the first round of the crisis, the urgency of the search for further ways of providing new sources of central bank liquidity has abated. Some proposals have been made for improving the quality of international bank portfolios, but they have received little official support. Central banks have been more concerned to proclaim the end of the crisis and express hopes that the system can now begin to function on a sounder basis.

One result of the events of 1982 is that over the next few years the World Bank and the International Monetary Fund will provide much more international credit. While sovereign debtors could obtain funds from the Euromarkets on minimal conditions, they were unwilling to seek to satisfy the IMF and the World Bank in order to borrow from them, but for some of these debtors these two multilateral institutions may now be the only source of long-term credit.

77

Impact of a sharp fall in the price of oil

It is possible that the next round of the banking crisis will happen even if the price of oil remains stable. Should the financial institutions be obliged once more to roll over their debt still further into the future and at the same time increase it so that the defaulting countries can again 'pay' interest payments on it, this could suffice to bring on the crisis. If a sharp fall in the price of oil were to occur and were seen to be likely to persist, the crisis would become inevitable, since most financial institutions would assume that the debt of large-scale borrowers who are oil exporters should be written off.

One or more, probably more, of the large Euromarket borrowers dependent on oil exports would default or - nearly the equivalent - impose a unilateral moratorium on principal and interest repayments on terms that would be unacceptable to its creditors. If a major debtor does this, then others will follow.

The rationale for such a default would be that the country concerned would have no expectation of benefiting from access to Euromarket funds in the foreseeable future and would therefore have little or nothing to lose from default. If this seems an extreme proposition, it is worth noting that the monetary authorities of the major OECD nations moved comparatively quickly to ease the rescheduling difficulties of such countries as Mexico and Brazil. They also supported intervention by the multilateral institutions on a large scale. It may be that they were simply concerned at the plight of the countries involved. A more likely explanation is that they recognized that either they support the debtors or they would be obliged to support, probably on a larger scale, their own banking institutions once the debtor nations had defaulted. The narrowness of the margin between default and an agreed debt rescheduling in 1982 suggests that if debtor countries are subjected to greater stress - for example through a sharp fall in the oil price - their reactions would be more extreme. It may well be that in these circumstances no sensible compromise could be reached between a country threatening default and the official financial institutions expressing some willingness to support it.

The position of debtors who import oil would improve substantially, but this offsetting factor would not be sufficient to stop a full-scale crisis. The perception of a sharp immediate deterioration in the quality of a large amount of bank debt would swamp any countervailing gradual improvement in another, smaller part of bank loan portfolios. If any less developed country repudiated its debt outright, the quality of all such debt would be seen to have worsened.

Once the first major debtor defaults, the political pressure on others to follow what would be seen as an anti-banking, anti-North strategy would become almost irresistible. If two or three of the major debtor nations default, then the credit standing of most important banks would be called into question, and their access to interbank funds and other sources of short-term funding would be sharply reduced. (An illustration of what could happen is given by the experience of Continental Illinois. When this bank's credit standing was called into question, the price of long-term debt that it had issued fell by some 15-20%. It had to issue short-term debt at rates well in excess of market rates. The deterioration in the net worth of Continental Illinois was on a much more limited scale than that which many major banks would experience in this scenario.)

It is necessary to maintain a sense of perspective: if the crisis occurs, it will almost certainly be resolved eventually by intervention by the monetary authorities of Europe, the USA and Japan; each will have to act to save its own major banks for domestic as well as international reasons. At the end of the crisis no large bank will have closed its doors, and banks will continue most of the international operations that they have developed over the past twenty-five years, though on a smaller scale.

Nevertheless, while the crisis lasted, markets would be unlikely to be reassured by the pronouncements of the regulatory authorities. The credit standing of the banks would deteriorate and non-bank institutions would not continue lending to the banks unless the interest rate charges reflected the risk they were taking. This risk payment during the 1982 banking crisis widened the differential between US government paper and US bank debt to more than 4 percentage points for three-month credit. This crisis would be more severe, and it is difficult to forecast the interest rate differentials that would develop.

One consequence of a banking crisis is that governments find it much easier to fund large deficits; there is a general willingness to purchase securities which have the guarantee of the national government. The other asset which enjoys general confidence in a banking crisis is of course gold, and an increase in its price to previous peak levels and beyond would be likely. (Gold currently at around $400 an ounce would, in this scenario, rise towards $1,000 an ounce.)

The scale and duration of the disruption in international

financial markets would determine the extent to which a large fall in the price of oil has an adverse impact on economic activity. At its worst the crisis could slow or halt the ability of international financial institutions to advance fresh funds to finance the growth in world trade and investment that most observers would expect to be associated with a fall in the price of oil. The institutions concerned would have to raise their margins on international lending sharply, since they would need to recover their costs on a much lower level of turnover (and would be seeking to restore their balance sheets through improved profitability). The market would sustain this increase in margins given the cutback in lending that the banks' poor balance-sheet positions would force on them. Put at its most simple, banks might demand from borrowers of intermediate financial standing a spread of 4-5% above the interbank interest rate as against the present spread of about 2%. This would impose heavy burdens on borrowers. Although they have faced higher total nominal interest-rate charges in the past, most notably in 1981 and 1982, the burden of such charges may have been less during a period of more rapid world inflation. (This approach - using the concept of 'real' interest rates - will have little appeal to primary producers, who saw commodity prices fall in those years.)

The international banks are, in general, either domestic banks or the subsidiaries of domestic banks. The deterioration in their credit standing would have an impact on their domestic business, since they would have to pay more to get the funds they require. It is likely that this impact would be smaller than the effects on their Euromarket lending. They would still find it necessary to cut back on domestic advances to reflect their poor balance-sheet positions and to seek to improve profit margins on domestic business to restore their net worth. Independently of action by monetary authorities there would be a tightening of monetary stance. The degree of tightening in monetary policy that took place in 1981 and 1982 was responsible for the world recession that is still under way. The deflationary impact of the tighter monetary stance that would be part of the next crisis would more than offset any of the longer-term reflationary consequences of the fall in the price of oil experienced as a result of the general changes in macroeconomic forces described above.

At best the monetary authorities of the OECD economies would move fast enough to constrain the destruction of confidence in the banking institutions caused by the default of the debtor economies. They would be able to limit the contraction of credit and the increases in interest rates described above. The development of other confidence-inducing mechanisms, such as loans by the IMF and additional credits offered by the World Bank, would also limit the adverse consequences of this sort of crisis.

Conclusion

It is normal to focus on the reflationary consequences of a falling oil price. Commentators argue that net importers of oil, who have large current account deficits, would find their balance-of-payments constraints eased and that they would be able to reflate. The impact of a weak oil price is now much less clear-cut given the need of many oil exporters to curb imports at present - so, for example, Brazil's improved export demand following an oil price cut could be partially offset by Mexico's emergency cuts in imports.

Once the possibility of a financial crisis following a sharp fall in the price of oil is taken into account, the prospect of limits on bank advances and the associated high interest rates could eliminate any potential stimulus to the world economy from a falling oil price.

6 OPEC

Louis Turner

The events of 1979-80 already seem like ancient history to OPEC's members. These were the years when its Long-Term Strategy Committee laboured to produce a formula for achieving predictable quarterly rises in the price of crude oil. They were also the years when Saudi Arabia strove intermittently to restrain the enthusiasm of other OPEC members for cranking up prices to the maximum that world markets would stand in the immediate aftermath of the Shah's fall and the subsequent Iran/Iraq war. Finally, these years saw considerable discussion within OPEC circles about the need to underpin oil prices by setting a group production ceiling of 30 - or even 26 - million b/d. Few observers foresaw that within three years demand for OPEC oil would be down to some 14 million b/d, and that the problem facing OPEC would be one of institutional survival, rather than one of sweeping success.

The March 1983 London Agreement thus poses a new set of questions. Some of these are too short-run to have a place here (such as whether oil price movements since then suggest that the agreement will last to the end of the year); others are of more lasting importance. For instance, should OPEC come under steady medium-term downward price pressures, what steps could it take to fight these over the next four or five years? And what foreseeable developments, within the OPEC grouping, will either strengthen or weaken its members' defensive strength over the years?

The problem of cohesion

Events leading up to the London Agreement suggest that OPEC's defensive position has significant weaknesses. First, until demand for OPEC's oil picks up substantially, the group is left with an overhang of production capacity of between 10 and 15 million b/d - an overhang which can only encourage price 'chiselling' by OPEC members. Second, the diplomacy in the year or so leading up to the London Agreement points to political splits within OPEC which are making cohesive decision-making particularly difficult. Iran's war with Iraq, and its active dislike of the conservative Arab oil states on the western side of the Gulf, have made Iran a distinctly disruptive force within OPEC circles. At a rather lower level of tension, Nigeria has not always seemed the happiest of bedfellows for the Middle Eastern oil producers.

Assuming, however, that the political will is there (an assumption to which I will return), then OPEC's immediate goals are clear. As a group, the OPEC oil producers have to maintain some form of prorationing system until demand for their oil picks up sufficiently to allow them to increase their export sales and, it is hoped, prices. The trouble with this goal is that OPEC has no convincing track record in this complicated area.

The conservative Gulf states did agree to coordinate limited production cutbacks in the period immediately preceding the fall of the Shah, but the Shah's fall meant that the agreement was never tested. Certainly, a loose agreement made at OPEC's March 1982 Vienna meeting to share a notional OPEC total of 17.5 million b/d had virtually no impact on individual members' production and pricing policies. The London Agreement is a less ambiguous deal, but problems still remain.

For one thing, it is becoming increasingly clear just how complex today's oil market actually is. A recent report[1], which was sympathetic to OPEC, suggested that there were the following forms of intra-OPEC competition:
- straight price discounts;
- extending credit terms;
- processing deals by which the crude exporter gets the income realized from final product sales, after refining and freight costs are deducted;
- barter deals;
- package deals, whereby crude oil is sold at official prices but is tied to sales of refined products or NGLs (natural gas liquids) at discounted prices;
- sales made on a c.i.f. basis (i.e. the seller absorbs the freight costs); and
- improved fiscal terms for those companies still with an equity stake in crude production.

To this list of mechanisms for price 'chiselling', one might add the observation that the increase in the volume of spot-market transactions since 1978 has introduced a further element of flexibility into oil markets which makes the task of monitoring any prorationing deal even more complicated.

There are two other considerations facing OPEC when it seeks to make any prorationing agreement stick. First, it must somehow keep the increasingly important non-OPEC oil producers in line. Second, it may even have to consider influencing price developments in non-oil energies such as gas and coal. In 1978-9, it was generally felt that the equilibrium price for oil would be set by the cost of coal liquefaction or gasification. Today, there is rather more awareness that the direct burning of coal and gas is a more important competitive force in the short and medium term. Therefore, the Soviet Union's gas-pricing policies, or the pricing interplay in the coal sector between Japan and, say, Australia, have an impact on demand for OPEC oil, and thus affect the success or failure of any prorationing attempt.

Intra-OPEC political control
The logic of this analysis is that OPEC's only chance of resisting strong downward pressures on oil prices is if some country, or group of countries, can assert control within the OPEC grouping, and thus assert authority on oil markets in general. The OPEC membership is not homogenous enough to be trusted to come up with the necessary initiatives. Countries such as Nigeria, Algeria, Libya, Iran and, sometimes, Venezuela have all followed policies in the past which can now be seen as having pushed the collective OPEC membership into supporting prices which are probably unsustainable. Too many OPEC members have been shown in the last couple of years as being willing to boost their individual exports on the apparent assumption that their actions would not bring the whole OPEC edifice crashing down. The situation now facing OPEC will probably not permit any further deviation from a common strategy on production and pricing. If oil prices do start moving downwards now, they could clearly fall a long way before reaching any natural floor.

In practice, it would appear that Saudi Arabia and the other states in the Gulf Cooperation Council (GCC) are seeking to play this guiding role within OPEC. With its vast reserves, Saudi Arabia is clearly well suited to play the role of swing producer for the other members of OPEC, though the latter have often fought the prospect of taking their lead from Saudi Arabia. In 1977, OPEC split on price levels, leaving Saudi Arabia and the UAE on a lower pricing tier. A similar development took place in the aftermath of the fall of the Shah, with the Saudis desperately trying to keep the rest of the OPEC membership from going over the $28 per barrel price level which the Saudis thought was appropriate. Price unification was finally agreed only in late 1981 (at a price now recognized as being too high).

Since then, Saudi Arabia has played a key role in staving off a complete oil price collapse. In a true swing producer role, it has allowed its oil production to plunge from 9.9 million b/d in 1981 to below 3.5 million b/d in early 1983. It was also Saudi Arabia, working with its GCC partners - Kuwait, the UAE and Qatar - at informal negotiations in Bahrain (January 1983), that put together the alliance within OPEC that made the London Agreement ultimately possible.

Assuming the London Agreement does come under further pressure, one would expect Saudi Arabia and its GCC allies to be the key in holding the line. For one thing, it has now formally accepted the role of swing producer in this agreement - a complete break from the past, when the Saudi authorities always insisted that oil production policies were a matter for them alone. For another, the GCC four are in the best tactical position within OPEC: between them, they have the financial reserves to withstand an oil price collapse longer than most, and they very definitely have the productive capacity to swamp the world oil market, driving the price down to whatever level they choose. They are therefore in a relatively strong position when dealing with countries like Nigeria which may be tempted to threaten the OPEC production-sharing scheme. On the other hand, there have to be questions raised about how much lower Saudi production can go below the 3.5 million b/d production level that is likely in the first half of 1983 before the Saudi position as swing producer becomes completely untenable. It has already had to cut its NGL exports below contracted levels, and Sheikh Yamani has warned that the fall in associated gas production is endangering the Kingdom's desalination and electricity generation needs.

In many ways, OPEC is lucky to have such a culturally cohesive group of countries as its core producers and exporters (though the political instability of the Gulf region is a matter of less satisfaction). This gives it far better prospects than those of most other attempts at producer cartels. On the other hand, the success of its efforts to stabilize oil prices does seem to rest on the speed with which demand for its oil rebounds in the future. If such demand does not pick up soon, then the strains within OPEC will grow again as the high absorbers start to be squeezed in a world in which oil prices cannot be raised, thus making price-shaving the only way to increase oil revenues (on the assumption that surreptitious price competition can produce more than compensatory increases in the volume of exports, at the expense of other OPEC members).

If OPEC's internal discipline does start to fray, then there is not a great deal that the GCC can do. As argued above, there may be physically determined limits to how far it can go in reducing production to make room for high-absorbing OPEC members. On occasion, it may be possible for the GCC producers to provide some temporary financial assistance to the more troubled OPEC members. In general, though, it looks as if the Gulf core of OPEC will be able to do little but try persuasion, with the ultimate threat that Saudi Arabia will, like Samson, bring the whole OPEC edifice crashing down on everyone's head. Like deterrents in some other fields of diplomacy, people may well assume that such a threat would never be carried out. The fact that it is only a half-credible threat may well make its eventual use more likely.

Controlling the non-OPEC world
If OPEC is going to have problems maintaining discipline within its own ranks, it will find it harder still to keep the non-OPEC competition under control. For the moment, it believes it has Mexico under its wing. Reports following the London Agreement refer to OPEC having 'achieved a very satisfactory degree of cooperation ... with Mexico'(2), with the latter having agreed to limit its export volume to 1.5 million b/d. Given that it is less than two years since Pemex under Diaz Serrano was proposing a $4 price cut in Mexican oil, one can understand why OPEC should be paying such close attention to a country which still seems able to increase production quite significantly.

It remains to be seen if OPEC can similarly coopt other smaller Third World oil producers like Egypt, Oman, Malaysia, the Ivory Coast and potentially Sudan. (This assumes that the oil industries of countries like Brazil and Argentina will primarily be for domestic consumption.) These are the kind of countries which are developing oil reserves precisely because they need the revenues, and they are unlikely to be keen to restrict production before they have established themselves in world markets - however much general sympathy they may have for OPEC as a champion of the Third World.

Cumulatively, these countries are of considerably less importance than those other potential mavericks, Britain and the Soviet Union. Clearly, OPEC's decision to hold its recent conference in London paid off by reminding the British authorities that collapsing oil prices would be a mixed blessing. In the medium term, though, one doubts if OPEC will prevail over the non-oil lobbies in Britain which have a vested interest in falling prices (providing they don't fall so fast they they wreck a significant part of the world's financial capacity). Undoubtedly, though, it is going to have to keep the diplomatic pressure on Britain, just as the decision to send an OPEC representative to discuss oil issues with the Soviet Union is a recognition that it is not only populous Third World oil producers which pose threats to long-term oil price stability.

In approaching Western exporters such as Britain and Norway, OPEC will clearly have to use some care, since there is considerable hostility to OPEC in the United States, and Britain is hardly likely to welcome transatlantic accusations that it has sold out to OPEC. OPEC, or its Gulf core, may be tempted to float proposals for new dialogues, but it is difficult to see how much use these might be. Undoubtedly, it can try to keep countries like Britain in line by threatening to reduce prices low enough to wreck the economics of North Sea production. Unfortunately for OPEC, this is really not a viable threat, since variable costs are a relatively small part of the overall cost of North Sea production, so it would have to cut prices to well below the $10 per barrel level to have much immediate impact on output (although development plans would be severely affected), and a relatively rich country like Britain, with a diversified economy, could survive with reduced oil revenues far better than a poor, undiversified oil producer such as Nigeria, Venezuela or Iran. In addition, a policy of aggressive price cuts would run the risk of producing retaliatory protectionist policies throughout most of the OECD world, as governments protected their relatively high-cost energy sectors such as coal and gas. At the end of such a price-cutting campaign, OPEC could find itself excluded from markets it once took for granted. It might well think twice before it decided to attack the Western oil industry head on.

What OPEC could clearly try to do is identify the price level which would win it back some 10 million b/d of lost markets, and thus, by bringing demand much closer to OPEC productive capactiy, it would clearly be in a far better position to discourage price competition among its members and to start edging prices up again as capacity limits were reached. Implicitly, this would be a price designed to discourage some marginal investments in fuel substitution, such as coal-for-oil schemes in industry, or to postpone investments in relatively expensive competitors to OPEC oil. Done subtly, it might well be able to strengthen its overall position. Done clumsily and aggressively, its current position as marginal supplier to the industrialized world could actually get worse.

The long run
It is hardly worth trying to make serious long-term forecasts of OPEC production because OPEC oil is now so much a marginal source of energy for the world(3) that one has to be confident about predicting the interactions of all other parts of the world energy sector before the OPEC figures can be calculated. For the moment, the range of recent forecasts has OPEC producing anywhere between 21 and 43 million b/d in the year 2000, at prices ranging from $28 to $98 in 1981-2 dollars(4). However, if we assume for the purpose of this study that prices stay low (presumably owing to a combination of relatively high energy efficiency and inter-fuel substitution away from oil, as well as perhaps lower than hoped for economic growth) a few conclusions can still be drawn.

First, if prices do stay low, then we can assume that OPEC will cease to exist as a price-setting force. The spending needs of a good part of its membership would at some stage lead to competitive export expansion, and consequently to the collapse of all price discipline. The OPEC grouping would become a price-taker rather than a price-maker.

Second, in a world of reasonably free energy trade, the countries currently making up the OPEC membership will remain in the oil business, though members with limited reserves, such as Qatar, Algeria, Indonesia, Nigeria and Venezuela, will either fade from the exporting scene in the coming decade, or else be much reduced exporters. The result will be that the low-cost, large-reserve countries such as Saudi Arabia, Iran and Kuwait (also Iraq?) will steadily increase their proportional importance within overall oil trade as smaller reserve countries start concentrating on just supplying their domestic markets. Their position may be strengthened as the international gas trade continues to expand, with both Iran and Saudi Arabia having the potential to become significant gas exporters as well.

There is thus no doubt that the Gulf members of OPEC will remain important, though it is far from clear that they will be able to re-establish a new, slimmed-down OPEC cartel based on the Gulf. Perhaps they will be able to, but so much depends on how far prices fall, and how fast demand for OPEC oil picks up, thus exhausting the marginal OPEC producers earlier rather than later. If there is a strong demand for oil and gas from this Gulf core some time in the 1990s, then this handful of countries may have the chance to resurrect the kind of central role for themselves that OPEC had during the 1970s. However, whatever the precise path followed by energy prices in the future, recreating the OPEC of the last decade will be difficult. The reason oil prices have moved downwards in recent months is that the entire energy sector has become more sophisticated and competitive and this new orientation is not going to be destroyed merely because oil prices stay low for ten years or so. Successful cartels tend to breed their own demise, and we are probably seeing the last defensive effort by OPEC before it loses control of the energy industry. The odds are that the oil market will come to behave more like those of other commodities such as copper - even though the oil sector will remain far more important than other commodities, both economically and strategically. However, the massive reactions to OPEC's success in the 1970s will ensure that it will be very much harder for any group of oil producers to capitalize a second time on a cyclical upswing in the industry to dominate it for another ten years. In the meantime, we wait to see if OPEC can fight off any further price declines. The odds are against it.

Notes
1. Middle East Economic Survey, 6 December 1982, pp.1, 2, 9.
2. Middle East Economic Survey, 21 March 1983, p.A6.
3. This argument is made in particular by Bijan Mossavar-Rahmani and Fereidun Fesharaki in OPEC and the World Oil Outlook: Rebound of the Exporters?, Special Report No. 140 (London, Economist Intelligence Unit, 1983).
4. Oil Prices in the Long Term: An Examination of Trends in Energy Supply and Demand and their Implications for the Price of Oil, a study by an interdepartmental group of officials (London, Department of Energy, 1982), Appendix, p.2.

89

7 Managing Energy Insecurity

Hanns W. Maull

We are not only confronting an oil surplus: we are confronting an international oil market that has undergone fundamental structural changes. This market has become less regulated and increasingly subject to market forces. The relationship between these two new developments is as yet unclear; it will no doubt vary over the coming years - with profound implications for energy security.

Important changes have taken place in market structures over the past four years: the amount of OPEC oil available to the majors has declined; the virtual disappearance of third-party sales and increases in direct sales by OPEC national oil companies and in government-to-government agreements have resulted in a proliferation of companies active in the international oil trade; the terms and lengths of contracts have altered; changes have occurred in refinery economics and product trade; and the importance of the spot market has become greater. The combined effect of these changes has been to emphasize the cyclical aspects of the international oil business. We therefore have to rethink energy security in terms of cyclical fluctuations.

Energy insecurity may be defined as 'dependence plus', as import dependence and vulnerability to supply disruptions and their implications. Vulnerability, in turn, has three main dimensions:

(a) the probability of supply disruptions of a certain magnitude (if the probability is very low, it might not be necessary to pay a large insurance premium);

(b) the ability or inability to absorb the shock of supply disruptions; and

(c) the broader economic and social costs resulting from inadequate adjustment to shortfalls.

Vulnerability can thus be seen as the mathematical product of (a) and (c), with (c) being determined by the size of the shortfall and the quality of crisis management and crisis instruments.

In the case of oil security, risks relate not only to supply shortfalls and their direct and indirect implications for economic performance, social consensus and political cohesion (nationally and internationally), but also to sharp price increases. As the second oil shock demonstrated, the costs of price explosions to OECD economies, and to the fabric of international economic cooperation as a whole, can be very dramatic indeed. Our ability to cope with supply shortfalls and their implications must apply to both types of risk if vulnerability is to be limited.

OPEC has always been the marginal supplier of energy. The growing importance of cyclical aspects in the international oil market is underlining this role. In 1979, OPEC accounted for 61% of free world oil production; in 1982, that share was down to 46%. While OPEC production declined by about 40% over this period, other non-communist oil production actually increased by some 10%. US data also illustrate the importance of the 'swing' phenomenon: in 1979, the United States consumed some 17.9 million b/d; total imports were about 6.8 million b/d or 38%, and OPEC imports were 5.3 million b/d, equivalent to not quite 30% of oil demand. In 1982, total consumption was down to an estimated 15.1 million b/d, imports were 3.9 million b/d or 26%, and OPEC imports had fallen to 1.9 million b/d or less than 13% of demand.

The structural changes affecting the supply of oil are particularly significant, but there are also structural changes influencing the demand for oil. To be sure, economic recession has been an important factor in the depressed levels of world oil consumption in 1981 and 1982; to some extent, therefore, economic recovery can be expected to lead to a surge in oil demand, particularly if we include restocking in the demand equation. There are, however, structural factors in the decline of oil consumption: more efficient use of oil, fuel-switching and changes in industrial production patterns have begun to make significant inroads in demand. The precise relationship between these structural causes and the cyclical (recession-related) causes for depressed levels of oil demand is something many people would dearly like to know. At present, all one can say is that an important part of the decline seems to have been due to economic recession, and that consequently there will be a cyclical upswing when the economy recovers, and hence some increased import dependence. But the underlying structural changes in demand, triggered by higher price levels, will continue.

According to two recent sets of projections for Western Europe - the OECD's low-growth scenario and that of Esso Europe - by 1990 West European oil import dependence will be between 27% and 29%, as compared to 43% in 1980(1). This is about the level of the year 1960. Structurally, therefore, import dependence will decline at least during the 1980s, and perhaps through the 1990s as well.

There are also reasons for assuming that effective demand (i.e. demand excluding stock changes at all levels) will tend to fluctuate less than in the past. This has to do with the changing composition of oil consumption. The greatest reductions will be in fuel oil used by industry; but it is industrial demand for oil which is most directly related to cyclical fluctuations in economic activity. This is borne out by a look at the fluctuations in product demand between 1973 and 1981. In Western Europe, for example, the ratio between the highest and the lowest consumption figures for gasoline was 1.17, for distillates 1.16, and for fuel oil 1.46(2). Similar figures can be observed for the US and the Japanese cases. With the decline in the share of fuel oil in total oil consumption (according to Esso(3), in Western Europe this share will go down from 33% in 1980 to 24% in 1990, and 22% in 2000, with total oil demand in the same period declining from 13.1 million b/d (1980) to 11.2 million b/d (both 1990 and 2000)), the overall fluctuations in oil consumption should be reduced.

Oil import dependence will thus fall significantly over the coming years. There will be cyclical ups and downs in the levels of dependence, but even these fluctuations could well become less pronounced.

Probability of supply disruption
How will the oil glut affect the probability of major supply disruptions? The answer to this queston depends on one's assessment of the implications of lower oil prices for producer countries' economic, social and political stability. The traditional distinction between 'high' and 'low' absorbers, which implies that most Arab Gulf producers will have little difficulty in weathering the glut, seems to me questionable. All producer countries will experience political strains in reducing levels of spending - although, of course, in differing degrees. Something which is often overlooked with respect to the Gulf producers of the Arabian Peninsula is that demand for petrodollars is not confined simply to economic requirements, such as development projects and imports for consumption: there are also equally important political pressures, both domestic and international, which have trad-

itionally been resolved through lavish spending. These include crucial special interest groups, such as members of the royal families, the armed forces, business; public expectations about the possibilities to get rich quickly and about appropriate welfare provisions; and vital foreign policy objectives, such as the support of Iraq against revolutionary Iran.

How governments will fare under these heightened pressures, will depend (a) on their flexibility and margin of manoeuvre, which, in turn, will depend on per capita income of oil, pretrodollar reserves and investment incomes, and (b) on the resilience and robustness of the political systems. It seems reasonable to conclude from this that falling oil revenues would increase the risk of supply disruptions as a result of political turmoil in producer regions - whether in the form of regional conflict or civil strife. The additional risk is perhaps greatest with regard to countries outside the energy heartland of the Gulf, since some of these countries will have to face declining export availability as well. This could make for a bumpy economic, social and political transition.

The glut factor and its implications for political stability in producer regions cannot, of course, be quantified: any developing country in a process of rapid transformation tends to be unstable rather than stable, and there are a number of other elements of instability in producer countries and regions. The net effect of falling oil sales and prices on the political stability of producer countries may therefore be quite small. If this is so, it would, however, reflect the underlying instability of a large number of oil-exporting countries and regions. One must therefore conclude that politically induced supply disturbances will continue to be quite likely, and that they could happen at any time. The implications of producer instability have to be measured in terms of their impact on the oil and energy situation and on the international political system. Again, the experience of the second oil shock and its aftermath should suffice to illustrate the point: the revolution in Iran changed the geopolitics and the very prospect for stability of the Gulf region, and even affected the broader structures of international cooperation and conflict between East and West.

Ability to cope with supply disruption
If a supply disruption does occur, the actual state of the market will matter. For the first line of adjustment consists in activating spare oil production capacity in areas that are unaffected by disruptive forces - and such spare capacity

would be available at times of glut. Indeed, it seems reasonable to assume that, given present production ceilings and capacities of OPEC members, there will be significant spare capacity during most of the 1980s. This is implied by OPEC's role as marginal or swing supplier - just as, again by implication, spare capacity outside OPEC will probably be quite limited. This raises the issue of OPEC's ability and willingness to activate spare capacity in a supply crisis. More precisely, one will probably have to ask this question for the Arab Gulf producers: the logic of the present prorationing agreement, and of the respective ability and flexibility of OPEC members to reduce exports, point towards a concentration of the marginal supply position in the Gulf, and largely in Saudi Arabia.

The Arab Gulf producers might, of course, themselves be affected by supply disturbances, and available spare capacity would then almost certainly be insufficient because (a) it would be relatively limited, and (b) the shortfall might be (or become) quite large. If they were not affected, they still might not be willing to allow their production to increase. This would be a political decision. Its motives could include:

- a desire to see oil prices go up in order to compensate for past losses in export revenues and to maximize short-term benefits;
- a reluctance to assist consumer nations and companies, which might be perceived as having made the most of the preceding glut 'without giving a damn for our interests'; and
- a reluctance to be seen assisting the United States because of the state of the Arab/Israeli conflict.

Again, the second oil shock might serve as an illustration of this problem: Saudi Arabia's production policy in 1979 was - perhaps not without relation to the Camp David Agreement and the Israeli/Egyptian movement towards a separate peace under US sponsorship - erratic and unclear, and this contributed to upward pressure on oil prices in spot markets.

The activation of spare capacity would be the most important contribution that producers could make to crisis management, but it is by no means their only instrument. Producer stockpiles, distribution flexibility through strategic pipelines, and control over tankers, destinations and shipping lines could all help in coping with shortages. This, too, would involve political clearance and active cooperation by OPEC members.

Consumer stockpiles are probably the most important instrument of crisis management available to importing countries. Again, superficially speaking, the lower levels of import demand associated with the oil glut will make a positive contribution to supply security: since import dependence is lower, smaller stocks would be sufficient to cover the same type of disruption. Indeed, the January 1983 position of stocks, with their coverage of more than 100 days of current IEA import demand, reflected this tendency. But this superficial contribution to oil security conceals two important problems: are stock levels sufficient to cope with a realistic worst-case scenario, and are stockpiling policies adequate?

To discuss this issue, one first has to distinguish between commercial and government-sponsored 'strategic' stocks of petroleum. In the case of the former, a large proportion of the inventories is needed to keep the oil distribution system running smoothly; these stocks are therefore not in fact available for serious crisis management. The effectiveness of commercial inventories as a buffer against supply distur-bances is particularly difficult to estimate at present, since the implications of structural changes in the market for 'normal' inventory levels have probably not yet become fully evident. I would speculate that there are two trends operat-ing at present: overall volumes of stocks could normally well be higher than before 1979 as a result of the proliferation of traders, and the changes in trade itself. On the other hand, the growing role of market mechanisms, competition and a reduced role for the majors could well have the effect of reducing the share of commercial stocks which could help to cope with unexpected major disruptions. The pressure on companies to cut down costs has certainly led to massive destocking, and to a redefinition of what constitutes minimum operating stock-levels. These pressures are likely to continue to operate, and thus to reduce the cushion of flexibility provided by commercial stocks.

A second issue of importance with respect to stockpiles is their increasing tendency to behave pro-cyclically: that is, to rise and fall as prices rise and fall. This again has to be seen as a consequence of structural changes in the market. As far as oil security is concerned, it will have a major multiplier effect in instances of supply disturbances: speculative and protective stockbuilding will tend to add to pressures on supplies and prices.

Both these trends indicate that, in the future, govern-ment-controlled stockpiles could well have to shoulder a larger burden of crisis management. The political psychology of oil gluts, however, is an important obstacle to formulating adequate stockpile targets and policies. In many consumer countries, strategic stockpiles are not even separated from commercial stocks; actual levels of strategic stocks could well be too low, depending on one's assumptions about worst-case risks, and there are no clear national, let alone international, understandings about how to use strategic stocks in an emergency to prevent severe dislocations and/or price explosions as a result of supply shortfalls. The IEA formula alone is patently insufficient to cover all types of serious risk.

Even more problematical is the degree of international cooperation between consumer countries that would be required for the successful management of a serious supply shortfall. Whether the United States would cooperate in the implementation of the IEA emergency allocation scheme has been doubted by many insiders. Its cooperation (and that of other countries) in a 'sub-trigger' crisis management operation must now appear equally uncertain. The glut will reinforce the belief that market forces (which in a glut are beneficial) can orchestrate the adjustment process. They can, of course. The question is, at what social and political, let alone economic, cost? The $1,000 billion loss of Gross OECD Product that resulted from OPEC II was, after all, also a result of the effective operation of market forces(4). And the formulation of policies for crisis protection will be pushed still further down the political agenda by falling oil prices and abundant supplies. This goes for national governments as well as for international organizations such as the IEA.

The ultimate line of adjustment to supply shortfalls therefore consists in demand restraint. Some lowering of consumption in a supply crisis has long been part of the IEA scheme. This should not provide great difficulties initially; in a prolonged crisis, however, the marked differences among OECD countries as regards both patterns of energy demand and administrative ability to impose restrictions on oil consumption could increasingly lead to tensions within the IEA. Once stocks are eroded or managed ineffectively, demand restraint will also come to imply economic and social hardship. The direct burden of adjustment will in the future tend to fall increasingly on the household and the transportation sectors - a result of the shifts in oil consumption patterns already outlined. This suggests that the absorption of shortfalls should become economically easier (the danger of the productive apparatus being adversely affected would be reduced) but politically more difficult (as adjustments would increasingly have to be made by individual citizens). The changes in consumption patterns will also reduce some of the layers of 'fat' in OECD oil consumption, which could easily be cut by fuel-switching. The implications of changes in consumption patterns are therefore somewhat contradictory. In any case, the impact of a serious supply shortfall will probably be determined, not by such underlying structural aspects as an economy's and a society's ability to absorb supply shortfalls, but by the politics and the psychology of crisis.

Prospects

In sum, then, one cannot be very confident about our ability to weather another oil crisis without severe implications for the political fabric of cooperation within and among OECD countries. Our effectively available stockpiles might be insufficient; we do not have a clear notion of how to use them; and whether there will be the necessary degree of political cooperation and compromise among IEA countries must remain doubtful. This conclusion is underlined by past experience: of the three major supply disruptions since 1973, only one (the most recent, a repercussion of the Iran/Iraq war) was managed successfully - which was as much by good luck as good management.

The implication of this is that the risks of major economic and social dislocations resulting from another supply disruption continue to be great. OPEC I and II have already weakened economic and political structures within and among OECD countries considerably; whether another major crisis would strain these structures beyond breaking-point is difficult to judge, but one certainly would not like to test the proposition. Much would depend, of course, on the actual crisis configuration. The risks of a major supply shortfall for a prolonged period have probably declined as a result of falling oil demand, for a number of reasons: OPEC's share of the market can be expected to be lower than in the past for much of the 1980s; there might have been a 'learning effect' for producers about the consequences of exaggerated price increases; capacity reserves should normally be available; and the lower levels of production and revenues of OPEC members make it more difficult to sustain a further reduction in exports, and less objectionable to expand production (concern with production ceilings will probably not play much of a practical role for the near future).

But all this does not imply that the probability of major disruptions has become negligible. One could distinguish between two types of risk now facing OECD countries: the first risk is a major, politically induced oil crisis in the Gulf. This would pose problems of price and of physical availability, and could totally transform a glutted market. The second type of crisis stems primarily from price effects, and could occur through a combination of a cyclical upswing and minor supply disturbances. The first type of contingency could hit us at any time; its management would be difficult under any oil market regime. On the other hand, the probability of such a crisis is perhaps not very great.

The second kind of contingency could hit us once demand starts to pick up, and inventories are built up again. If something unexpected then aggravates market pressure, spot prices could well move up sharply, leading to a general escalation of price levels. Given the importance and variability of stock movements, it is not inconceivable that some political event (say, an escalation of hostilities between Iran and Iraq or a new Saudi oil policy, with a production ceiling of 5 million b/d) could in itself produce the turnaround in oil demand without any immediate and direct effect on the supply side. That is to say that this second kind of emergency could also hit us earlier than we might expect.

In conclusion, it seems to me that changes in the oil and energy outlook in no way justify a relaxation of our efforts to build up adequate insurance against the great political, social and economic costs which another oil crisis could imply. In fact, our present insurance policies seem by and large inadequate. Levels of strategic stockpiles might well be insufficient; the organization and management of stockpiles leaves something to be desired in several IEA countries; and there are no effective policies for stock drawdowns in the case of a threatening oil price explosion.

I would also regard the structural changes in the oil market as being an issue of economic security: the variability and cyclical fluctuations implied by these changes represent in themselves significant risks. The international oil market is simply too important to be left to market forces. If oil prices were to decline further, and if they were thought likely to continue to decline for a longer period, then this might lead to a reversal of the present trends towards greater efficiency of oil use and towards fuel-switching. 'Gas guzzlers' are already making a comeback in US automobile sales, and cheaper fuel oil could hamper efforts at conversion in industrial boilers. Lower prices could also endanger adequate investment in alternative energy projects and more expensive sources of oil. The net result could then be a replay of the past, with mounting pressure on OPEC supplies as the cheapest and most readily available source of large quantities of energy.

Such a development could be checked only through mechanisms which contain the decline in effective prices to oil consumers. This could be achieved in several ways: through forceful and cohesive action by OPEC, through coordination and cooperation between producer and consumer governments, and through taxes on crude oil imports or products within the OECD countries. Such taxes would probably have to be coordinated among the OECD members so as to avoid a distortion of relative competitiveness of industrial production with a high energy component, if they were to apply to crude oil or all products. Additional taxes have certainly been under discussion in the United States and in the European Communities; their effect would be to shift back effective market control to consumer countries. Finally, prices might even stabilize through the interplay of market mechanisms with limited OPEC efforts to maintain prices - but the structural changes in the industry sketched in Chapter 8 make this less likely than in the past.

Some measure of political intervention will thus probably be necessary to protect OECD economies from a repeat of excessive reliance on OPEC oil. We are coming round to accept political intervention to even out erratic market movements in the international monetary system; this lesson will probably also have to be learnt in the case of oil. At the same time, it is at present extremely difficult to see how control over the market could be strengthened. At the moment, none of the theoretically conceivable types of control - through OPEC, through the companies, through consumer cooperation, or through cooperation between these groups of actors (for example, through a producer-consumer dialogue) - looks very realistic.

Notes

1. IEA, World Energy Outlook (Paris, OECD/IEA, 1982); Esso, Energy in Europe, Looking Forward to the Year 2000 (Brussels, Esso, December 1982).
2. BP Statistical Review of World Energy 1981 (London, BP, 1982).
3. Esso, op. cit.
4. IEA, op. cit.

8 The Oil Industry

Adrian D. Hamilton

Those seeking an explanation for the extraordinarily nervous
and volatile behaviour of the oil markets during 1983 need
look no further in some ways than the behaviour of the oil
companies. Ever since the 1973 crisis, and the heated
political confrontation between the major oil companies and
individual consumer governments, the international oil groups
have been saying that they no longer had the power or the
commercial incentive to act as a stabilizing force in the oil
trade.

In the second oil shock of 1979, with the fall of the Shah,
they - or at least a number of them - showed that they
meant it when it came to an outright crisis of supply
shortage. Now, the majority of them have shown that they
mean it in a crisis of surplus. In an astonishingly rapid space
of a year or even less, nearly all the majors have cut back
their long-term contracts for oil and have concentrated
instead on short-term purchases(1). Subsidiaries have been
left free, and have been actively encouraged to gain the best
deals that they can and to play the market. Purchase
agreements from producer countries, most notably Nigeria,
have been interpreted in minimum instead of maximum
terms, and oil companies - Gulf in the United Kingdom, for
example - have shown themselves quite prepared to refuse to
purchase and to walk away from long-standing supply agreements if the price was not right. Oil company actions on
stocks and purchases have tended to heighten the volatility of
the market, not suppress it. BP's unprecedented intervention
in the OPEC debate in London last March, when it publicly
warned that agreement would be impossible if the price of
North Sea oil was not reduced to below that of Nigeria, was
an indication not only of BP's peculiar dependence on North
Sea profits but also of its very real concern that it would
have to undermine the agreement if even the minutest
differentials were not established satisfactorily. If the first

quarter of 1983 witnessed every force combining in one direction - warm weather, destocking, falling demand - then the effect of oil company decisions was to add to the pressure, not restrain it.

Nor could companies have acted otherwise. Having sought, pleaded and argued for a generation for release from political controls and government intervention, they have found a market far freer than any of them could have envisaged only a few years ago, and not altogether to their liking - as falling demand, weakening prices, dramatic surpluses in both producing and processing capacity and intensifying competition have put all the same pressures on oil companies as they have on the steel, automobile and more nearly related chemical industries.

And, like those businesses, the oil companies have had to react by pruning their loss-makers, concentrating on marginal profit, curbing investment and acting far more like traders. As chairman after chairman of the major oil companies has repeatedly said over the past year or more: no longer can a company look at its business as an integrated whole or regard its primary duty as the guarantee of supply at all costs. Each part of the business must stand or fall on its own commercial merits - a simplification perhaps, but a real enough reversal of the old justification of the major oil companies as integrated, international intermediaries between producer and consumer, ironing out the short-term fluctuations of the market and investing long-term to ensure the oil would be available whenever it was needed.

The question that faces the oil industry, and hence its customers, is what kind of trading structure will this brave new world of competitive short-term trading produce, and whether indeed it is the shape of the future or simply a short-term response to short-term pressures.

Has oil become like any other commodity, to be traded and invested in and to experience the repercussions of fluctuations in world trade as do, for example, copper or cocoa? Or does it remain a special commodity with different market rules, different political intervention and hence a unique structure to handle it? For the oil companies it is a far more important question than how far and how fast oil prices will fall, much though this may have mesmerized the markets and the financial institutions for the time being.

The significance of lower prices
Not that the direction of prices is unimportant. No more than anyone else had the oil industry planned for, or

101

expected, a fall in oil prices at this time. Some oil companies, most perhaps, have been rather more cautious than governments in assuming a substantial real price increase for energy as the implication of the oil shocks of the 1970s. Few since the last oil shock of 1979 have based their investments on the premise of higher real prices. But nearly all oil and energy companies have accepted almost as an article of faith that price increases would keep pace with inflation through the 1980s and probably well into the 1990s as well. And to that extent the current market reversal must, and is already, causing a change in investment assumptions and corporate fortunes.

Even before prices started to fall, the rapid downward revision of demand forecasts that began to develop in companies from 1981 onwards induced them to slacken the pace in constructing major new processing facilities, whether to make oil from shale, tar sands or even coal. Almost all the major oil companies have now withdrawn from high-cost shale oil and tar sand projects. The main effect of actual price falls, coming on top of this, has been to savage the smaller exploration companies that had mushroomed as a result of US oil price deregulation; but even large oil companies must, whether admitted or not, have been obliged to reconsider oil investment, if only because their own cash flow has been constrained by collapsing demand and competition at the pump.

But price levels alone, however low, will not greatly alter the structure of the oil industry so long as the same prices apply to all competitors. Indeed a collapse in prices could actually restore traditional structures by wiping out the newcomers and the pure exploration or trading companies and leaving more of the business in the hands of the major oil companies with their greater financial resources, their continued ties with the low-cost producers of the Gulf and their greater efficiencies of scale (depending of course on whether governments would allow this reversion to the days of Standard Oil). At $25 per barrel, few oil companies would invest in deep-water oil. At $20 per barrel, offshore investment and deep drilling would be severely curbed, but existing investments would continue. At $15 the threshold for new investment would again be lowered. But the traditional oil companies would survive because they have the investment in place.

No oil group would welcome a precipitate fall in the price of oil - no business ever likes volatility in the cost of its basic raw material, although most industries have had to learn to live with it over the past decade or so. But it is perhaps significant that Peter Walters of BP has been alone among oil company chairmen in publicly warning of the dangers of a price fall and in his continued belief that the trend in real prices is still upwards through the rest of this decade and century. Other companies may hope that he is right. But a number - Shell among them - have been reworking their figures to look at the possibility of no real price increase from now on and even a small price fall. And although they do not like it, they feel they can live with it.

Indeed it could be argued that the real squeeze of falling prices is felt initially not by the oil companies but by host governments. For it is their tax revenues that tend to suffer most from falling prices, the more so since so many of them raised marginal taxes on oil in order to gain the maximum economic rent from the so-called 'windfall' increase in profits arising from higher prices. And it is governments that have the difficult choice of trying to hang on to much-needed oil revenue or of easing the burden of taxes on companies to encourage them to sustain investment when market conditions become less attractive.

What the price debate has done, however, is to intensify the existing debate within the industry about which course the international integrated companies should follow. Should they continue internationally, or should they go for whatever offers them the best profits? Should they act as traders and continue special and long-term relationships with individual producers? Is it oil or other investments that will provide the growth in future earnings through this century and beyond?

One should always be wary of dramatic options. Crises have a way of making long-standing contradictions seem novel and suggesting there are alternatives when longer-term trends have already determined the course. There has always been a tension in oil comapnies between the long-term planners, with their careful - and now much-derided - forecasts of supply and demand, and therefore of investment opportunity, and the commercial operators with their response to marginal opportunity. At any one time during the 1960s it was freight rates or access to Libyan oil or Groningen gas that distinguished the competitive results of companies and on which their boards spent far more time than on longer-term questions. During the 1970s it was stock positions and access to the so-called 'Saudi advantage' that determined results. During the 1980s it has been freedom from high-cost equity oil (oil which the companies own themselves) that has so far made the most impact.

The dominance of the majors

In a very real sense the tremendous expansion of oil trade in the post-war years has been dominated, and effected, until surprisingly recently by the unique structure of a business in which a few major oil companies - the 'Seven Sisters'(2) - handled the bulk of oil going into international trade, pushing their equity oil from the Gulf and OPEC sources through their international chains of transport, refining and marketing facilities, and financing a quite extraordinary degree of their investment from their own earnings. As late as 1971 the Seven Sisters owned over 60% of the non-communist world's crude oil, compared with 30% held by other private companies and less than 10% by the governments of the producer countries. When the United States is excluded, the figures become considerably greater - at nearly three-quarters of oil owned by the majors. And the same was true of product sales. In 1971 the seven major companies between them accounted for 54% of product sales in the world outside communist areas, compared with 36% handled by other private companies and only 10% by state companies(3).

It was a system that always had its critics, who argued that the price to the consumer would have been much lower and much nearer the actual cost of production in the Middle East had it not been for government protection in the United States and this control by the major oil companies, with their natural interest in combining with OPEC to keep a structured price pattern. But the point for most consumers was that it got the job done, fitted with the pattern of an industry whose incremental supply was coming from a limited area of the Middle East, whose logistics, like those of many other industries, were dominated by economies of scale, and, not least, whose immense capital investment needs were being met from within the industry.

The last decade has effectively destroyed this control and destroyed it for good. At the producing end of the business, the most obvious agent, ever since 1969, has been nationalization. By 1981, the share of the non-communist world's crude oil owned by the majors had been halved, to barely more than 31%, and the share held by other private companies had fallen to 21%; the governments of producing countries, by contrast, had increased their ownership to nearly half, at 48% of the non-communist world's supply and 70% of all oil outside North America. There were still advantages to equity oil, as the four partners in Aramco (Exxon, Mobil, Texaco and Standard Oil of California) found during the years of comparative price advantage for Saudi oil at the turn of the decade. And companies hung on surprisingly long to equity oil, partly because of nervousness among producers over selling oil themselves. But in general the industry recognized the end of equity oil and acted accordingly from early on in the last decade.

At the marketing end of the business, the hold of the majors has continued longer. By 1981, the majors still handled more than 40% of the product sales of the non-communist world, while state marketing companies, although doubling their share, still handled barely more than a fifth. And this figure is unlikely to be much higher today.

But even here the majors have had difficulties. The investment surge in non-OPEC sources which the oil companies had hoped to lead was constricted by government control, as in Mexico and Norway, or by heavy taxation and confused administrative control, as in the United Kingdom. Nor was the market much better. An important reason for the comparative slowness of state oil companies to expand in the market over the past five years has been the lack of profit in a business increasingly dominated by overcapacity in refining.

For the oil companies, the question has been not so much whether for the foreseeable future oil would continue to be the world's most important internationally traded commodity (it clearly will) as whether they would be allowed a role, and how they should prepare for the day when other fuels would take over the energy mix. Fears of nationalization and the role of state oil companies, resentment over tax rates and doubts about whether diversification would be confined to other energy sources or would go outside dominated the industry's thinking.

Some companies (notably Gulf) decided to retreat from an international role, since the nationalization of equity oil had removed the incentive which had encouraged them to expand in Europe in the first place. Others (notably Shell) decentralized into national rather than internationally integrated units. Mobil, on the other hand, concentrated on business streams, with companies involved in production, marketing, transport and, especially, exploration on an international scale. All took advantage of short-term high earnings from the immediate shocks of 1973, and even more 1979, to diversify into coal, minerals and even unrelated areas of electronic office equipment (Exxon) and retailing (Mobil). What none doubted within the oil and energy business was that future demand would require more expensive and more exotic sources, whether in shale oil and deep-water production or in oil from coal or gas. What none equally doubted was that their role could no longer be to carry the major burden of the oil trade. They would each have to go their own way, forced as much by the sheer cost of the next stage of development and the end of traditional economies of scale as by their reading of future supply-and-demand curves and political intervention.

Future relations between government and industry

For governments, this undoubtedly raised a difficult problem. If the oil industry, as it clearly showed in 1979, was no longer prepared to act as the international crisis manager, then governments had to decide how far they themselves should step in, either in cooperation (the IEA) or individually, to control production, to effect import security through barter or other deals and to regulate the industry.

A fall in oil prices obviously changes some of this thinking, in some ways to the benefit of the industry. It makes the market considerably less attractive to governments, both producer and consumer governents, as the French have found in their relations with the Algerians, the Japanese in their relations with the Iranians and the Libyans in their relations with the Italians. So long as prices remain 'soft', governments will tend not to expand their share of the oil business, and some rapprochement between the oil companies and OPEC may occur.

For the oil companies, lower prices will tend to accelerate rather than change the course of developments. The biggest single factor in recent oil company thinking has been the continuous downward revision of demand. The consequent reconsideration of large-scale investments in projects that were basically aimed at meeting a supposed gap in the medium-term future (synthetic oils from coal or shale) and the withdrawal from areas of surplus processing capacity (Europe especially) will be speeded up, as the recent Gulf Oil and Chevron offers for sale of their European refining and marketing facilities have indicated.

By 1985 the Seven Sisters' old dominance will be altered beyond recognition, as commercial pressures take their toll. It is possible to foresee an industry in which only Exxon and Shell remain truly international in scope and balanced in investment. Gulf will have retreated largely to North America. Others will have retreated from large areas of marketing or business, such as chemicals. It is the gap left on one side by an oil industry induced by commercial pressures to leave the international trading scene and on the other by governments reluctant to enter it for fear of commercial disaster which should concern the consumer.

If the present weakness reflects a permanent and fundamental change in the nature of the oil market, the end of oil's
separate status, there is no problem. If one assumes that oil
is now like any other commodity, with no long-term supply
problems, then the more the industry is fragmented and the
less part governments play the better. The adoption by the
international oil companies of a more purely trading role can
only be for the better, and their retreat from large-scale
investments will only be the inevitable consequence of a
market which no longer requires such large investments to
ensure that demand can be met.

If, however, it is the case that oil remains too strategically important and its fundamental supply constraints too
basic for its management to be left in the hands of the short-
term market, then the past year of activity by the oil
companies gives cause for concern. Of course companies
have not changed attitudes completely. Groups such as Mobil
persisted in their belief in the value of long-term contractual
relations with Gulf producers. Shell and Exxon have
increased rather than reduced capital expenditure and they,
like others, still have a foot in the door of synthethic fuels
research and develoment should the market open up again. If
current commercial pressures make oil a more difficult
business, they also make diversification less lucrative. But
the industry's tendency to confine its crude oil purchasing to
short-term contracts, its more ruthless attitude to stocks and
its withdrawal from big project investment has served to
intensify the uncertainties of the market and the swings in
price and supply.

In a world where the banks and international financial
institutions are taking a harder view of Third World investment and where governments are cutting public expenditure,
oil still demands high-cost risk investments. These, in turn,
require an appropriate industrial structure and a modus
vivendi between governments and companies to ensure that
investment and security of supply are maintained.

As ever, this modus vivendi will be influenced as much by
the policies of government as by the pressures of the market.
In one sense, the present situation can but tip the balance of
negotiating power between government and companies a
little in the companies' favour. Especially in the area of
exploration, governments will now have to compete more for
industry investment. This in turn will be reinforced by the
trend of international lending institutions such as the World
Bank and IMF to favour co-financing - joint institutional and

107

private capital - in new loans. The Philippines and China are examples of countries which are now anxious to see exploration investment undertaken and which are ready to offer more attractive terms to get it. The international companies, the bogeymen of the past, are now being made respectable again in the developing world, although whether the companies themselves will respond depends in no small part on the counter-attractions of a decontrolled North America.

The really interesting question over the next ten years, however, will be how the major developed nations will respond to the changed market circumstances for oil. For they now have economic as well as strategic imperatives to complicate their thinking. In the first place, the ten years since 1973 have seen the emergence of a number of major oil and energy producers in the ranks of the industrialized world. Of the 24 member states of the OECD, half have oil and gas resources of their own which are currently under development - Australia, Canada, Denmark, Germany, Ireland, the Netherlands, Norway, Spain, Turkey, the United Kingdom and the United States. And, of these, Australia, Canada, the Netherlands, Norway and the United Kingdom are all substantial oil or gas exporters or potential exporters. It is hardly surprising that Britain should be so ambivalent about a fall in oil prices or that it should act so quickly to ease tax terms on the North Sea. (Its terms, since the 1983 budget, are probably now the most attractive anywhere in the world outside the United States.)

In the second place, even those countries without indigenous production have now invested heavily in programmes to ease their import dependence, whether it is France's nuclear power programme or New Zealand's decision to produce petrol from its natural gas using the methanol route. Should there be a collapse in oil prices, there is bound to be a call for additional taxes on energy, whether in the form of an import fee (as in the United States) or a consumption tax (as in the EEC) to protect those investments. The trade-off between the benefits of lower oil prices to inflation and the need for protection is a sensitive one, determined as much by political as by economic calculations. Even short of a collapse in prices, it is possible to see governments taking more discreet action to protect their domestic investments, and their domestic industries.

In doing so, they would seem bound to accelerate the fragmentation of the international industry. Yet the usefulness of a basic element in the oil market which is capable and interested in long-term investment, in maximizing supply sources and in smoothing out price cycles becomes all the greater as the market becomes more cyclical. Should there be another oil crisis, or another sharp hike in prices, there will be little to protect the importing world from its full blast. Governments will have to step in, or make it worthwhile for the industry to do so.

Just as governments needed oil companies in the past to protect them from short-term strains in the oil market, oil companies in the future may need governments to protect them from the same short-term fluctuations.

Notes

1. Sir Peter Baxendell, chairman of Shell, suggested in a speech at Surrey University, 15 April 1983, that 30-40% of all crude handled by the majors was coming from short-term sources rather than from the companies' own output on longer-term contracts, compared to 5-10%, at most, ten years ago.
2. Royal Dutch/Shell Group; Exxon; Gulf Oil; Mobil: Standard Oil of California; Texaco; BP.
3. All figures from Shell's Energy in Profile, Shell Briefing Service, No. 6, 1982.